The LAMP SHADE BOOK

Art Direction: Celia Naranjo
Photography: Evan Bracken, Light Reflections
Editorial Assistance: Laura Dover
Illustrations: Charlie Covington
Technical Assistance: Scott Kenyon, The Lamp Shop;
  Jodi Blankemeyer, GE Lighting
Proofreading: Julie Brown

Library of Congress Cataloging-in-Publication Data
Cusick, Dawn.
    The lamp shade book : 80 traditional & innovative projects to
    create exciting lighting effects / by Dawn Cusick.
        p.   cm.
    Includes index.
    "A Sterling/Lark book."
    ISBN 0-8069-8154-7
    1. Lampshades. 2. Painted lampshades. I. Title.
    TT897.C86   1996
    745.593'2—dc20   96-22387
                                                      CIP

10 9 8 7 6 5 4 3 2

A Sterling/Lark Book

Published by Sterling Publishing Co., Inc.
387 Park Avenue South, New York, NY 10016

Created and produced by Altamont Press, Inc.
50 College Street, Asheville, NC 28801

© 1996, Altamont Press

Distributed in Canada by Sterling Publishing,
        c/o Canadian Manda Group, One Atlantic Ave., Suite 105, Toronto, Canada M6K 3E7
Distributed in Great Britain and Europe by Cassell PLC
    Wellington House, 125 Strand, London WC2R 0BB, England
Distributed in Australia by Capricorn Link (Australia) Pty Ltd., P.O. Box 6651, Baulkam Hills, Business
Centre, NSW 2153, Australia

Printed in Hong Kong

ISBN 0-8069-8154-7

The Lamp Shade Book

80 Traditional
& Innovative
Projects to
Create Exciting
Lighting Effects

Dawn Cusick

DESIGNER CREDITS

A special thanks to the following designers who contributed projects.

LEE ANDRE owns a mural and decorative painting business serving commercial and residential customers in Seattle, Washington. She is coauthor of *Decorative Painting for the Home* (Sterling Publishing, 1994).

CAROLYN PIEPER-BENFORADO enjoys working with fabric in sculptural ways. She owns Individuality, an apparel design and fabric arts company in Madison, Wisconsin.

JOYCE CUSICK is a lace collector and designer living in Dunnellon, Florida. She owns Historic Preservation, Inc. and is the author of *Crafting with Lace* (Sterling Publishing Co., 1993).

FRED TYSON GAYLOR taught art for ten years in the community college system and has worked as a product designer for domestic and international manufacturers and importers. He is a frequent contributor to craft books.

DIANE GRINNELL is a textile designer and fiber artist living in New York City. Her current work involves marketing textiles and prints to apparel and home furnishing companies as well as researching textiles and paintings for international and domestic auctions.

BOBBY HANSSON recently retired from a 30-year photography career in New York City. He now resides in Rising Sun, Maryland, where he operates the Leaping Beaver Tinker Shop. He is the author of *The Fine Art of The Tin Can* (Lark Books, 1996).

SCOTT KENYON owns and operates The Lamp Shop, an international retail and wholesale mail order company offering a complete selection of products for the lamp shade crafter. For an 18-page catalog, send $2.50 to The Lamp Shop, Department L, P.O. Box 3606, Concord, NH, 03302-3606.

MARY MAXWELL has been making one-of-a-kind Victorian shades for almost 20 years. She shares her how-to expertise through a series of video tapes available through her company, Hart Enterprises, in Roseville, California.

MARY MCCLAREN is a jewelry designer, button fanatic, and architect living in Phoenix, Arizona. Mary tries to go beyond embellishment, getting viewers involved in her work by inserting unsubtle messages.

GENE MESSICK teaches film writing, photography, and stained glass making throughout the Southeast. He markets his stained and fused glass work through his company, Lightworks Studio, in Shelby, North Carolina.

MARY JANE MILLER is a full-time studio artist working in decorative painting, woodworking, and a range of other techniques. She lives half the year in Abingdon, Virginia, and the other half in Mexico.

LEAH NALL left a fast-track career in broadcast news in Los Angeles for a rural life in Fairhope, Alabama. Her companies, Shadeworks and Needleworks, specialize in custom lamp shades and home sewing.

CHRIS NOAH-COOPER specializes in cut and pierced paper lamp shades, Scherenschnitte, etchings, and faux finished frames. An art teacher and art therapist, her work has appeared in *Better Homes and Gardens*. She resides in Miamisburg, Ohio.

KATHY OLER recently left a career as a teacher and university administrator to pursue a life in art. She is currently exploring works in fiber and photography, searching for marriages between processes and products. She resides in Lubbock, Texas.

CAROL PARKS is a sewing and craft book editor/author living in Asheville, North Carolina. Her former guest bedroom and closets overflow with fabric and other raw materials, a reflection of Carol's determination to support the national fiber economy.

MARION PECK is a fine arts painter from Seattle, Washington. Her work is displayed in galleries both nationally and internationally.

OLIVIER ROLLIN is a French multimedia artist currently residing in Asheville, North Carolina. He creates and markets a variety of custom light sculptures through his business, Olivier Rollin Designs.

PAT SCHEIBLE, a former research biologist, keeps busy with trompe l'oeil and faux finish work for commercial and residential clients in the Southeast. She lives in Mebane, North Carolina.

ANN SIBERLICHT owns and operates To Dye For in Silver Spring, Maryland. She specializes in handpainted silk and decorative accents for the home.

JONATHAN STUCKY, a multimedia textile artist specializing in quilts, lives in Western North Carolina. He enjoys working on community art projects such as the opening of The Rock and Roll Hall of fame and children's art programs.

GINGER SUMMIT is a former teacher living in Los Altos Hills, California. Ginger enjoys all forms of designing and crafting with gourds. She is coauthor of *The Complete Book of Gourd Crafts* (Lark Books, 1996).

SUZANN THOMPSON learned to knit at age seven and to crochet at 12. She has published knit, crochet, and jewelry designs in many craft publications, is contributing editor to Jewelry Crafts magazine, and works for Monsanto's Designs for America program. She will soon be living in Sheffield, England.

KIM TIBBALS is a frequent contributor to craft books. She enjoys drawing, sewing, gardening, herbal crafting, and broom making. She resides in Waynesville, North Carolina, where she is pursuing a second career as a dental hygienist.

SANDY WEBSTER is a fiber artist whose work has appeared in national publications and juried exhibitions. She frequently teaches basketry and jewelry workshops and gives inspirational lectures on art-related subjects.

E. ANN YANCY owns and operates Yancy Designs, a custom lighting and home accessories company in Charleston, South Carolina. Many of Ann's designs are inspired by her childhood love of box kites and her interest in Japanese lanterns.

Portfolio images were contributed by the following designers.

Norman Bacon, 105 Wittenberg Road, Bearsville, New York, 12409.

Judy Dykstra-Brown and Bob Brown, 1060 Nina Court, Boulder Creek, California, 95006.

Carter Clough, 1810 N. Garrett #112, Dallas, Texas, 75206.

Laura Goldberg, 1611 Eastwood, Highland Park, Illinois, 60035.

Ben Goldstone, 934 45th Avenue, Oakland, California, 94601.

Lisa Graves, 874 41st Street, Oakland, California, 94608.

Billy Hall, 16708 Green Dolphin Lane, Huntersville, North Carolina, 28078.

Sue Johnson, 1745 Solano Avenue, Berkeley, California, 94707.

Erik van Lennep, Post Office Box 73, Strafford, Vermont, 05072.

Gene Messick, Lightworks Studio, 147 Lawing Road, Marion, North Carolina, 28752.

Andrew Olsen, Post Office Box 23032, Richmond, Virginia, 23223.

William C. Richards, Clay Canvas Designs, Post Office Box 361, Underwood, Washington, 98651.

Olivier Rollin, 33 Carolina Lane, Asheville, North Carolina, 28801.

Cynthia Wynn, 37 Biltmore Avenue, Asheville, North Carolina, 28801.

CONTENTS

INTRODUCTION

Most lamp shades live their lives as the ultimate wallflowers, quietly diffusing and directing light, with rarely a second look ventured their way. Ask a lamp shade to dance, however, and the world lights up.

Add color to a room with simple fabric or decorative paper shades. Add texture with piercing or cutting. Or transform a shade into a miniature work of art with painting, stenciling, or collage. Punctuate your favorite decorating style with sundry trims, creating an eye-catching focal point of the room.

The dancing shades in this book are designed to suit all craft levels and a variety of time investments. If you want a finished shade tonight, stop by a discount or lighting store, purchase a well-shaped shade, and work from there.

If time is not an issue, search out discarded shades, remove everything down to the frame, and start from scratch for pennies. Or, search out the perfect frame from a well-stocked lamp shade supply company and create a masterpiece.

Choose to replicate the designs presented in this book or combine several with your imagination for a custom look. However you choose to work, once you've noticed lamp shades, they'll become one of your favorite dance partners.

BASIC LAMP SHADE CRAFTING

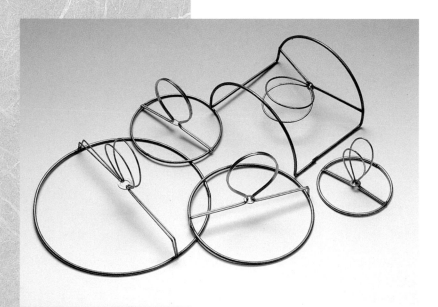

Top shade rings fitted to clip directly onto light bulbs.

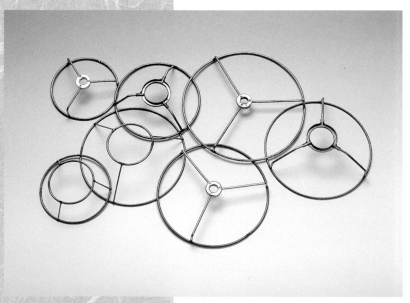

Top shade fitter rings for use with harps and finials. This type of hardware can be converted into clip tops with special clip adapters.

Fortunately, there's nothing mysterious about lamp shades and bases. Just take a peek inside of the next ten lamp shades you come across and you'll have a fairly good idea of how they work. Shade material (usually fabric or paper) is adhered to a frame (top and bottom support wires connected with vertical struts) or by top and bottom wire forms that are held in place by the shade. The finished shade sits down on top of a structure created by the lamp base (known as a harp) with the two parts secured by a finial, or the top ring comes with a clasp to fit around the bulb.

For most of the projects in this book, you can work with an existing shade or make your own from scratch. When shopping for a prospective shade, take a good look at its surface and ask yourself if it's compatible with the decorating technique used in your chosen project. How thick is it?

(Shades that are too thick won't work for cutout projects.) How porous is the surface? (Fine paintbrush strokes will bleed if the surface is too porous.) Is the color dark or light enough for surface design techniques?

The second option, making your shades from scratch, is admittedly more work, but gives you infinitely more creative control. If you have a very specific idea of what you want, you could easily spend more time shopping for the perfect shade than it would take to make it. For crafters who plan to make several custom shades as gifts or to market at craft shows, the added expense of purchased shades can dampen creativity.

Keep an open mind when shopping for materials. Fabrics can be backed with styrene (an adhesive plastic with a peel-away backing) or with a fusible knit interfacing to add stiffness. Lamp shade supply companies offer an attractive variety of prelaminated fabrics. Virtually any type of

A sampling of decorative and functional lamp shade parts. The finials (far right, top to bottom) can be used as is or decorated to match your shade with any number of surface design techniques. Other helpful gadgets include socket risers (for use when a clip-on shade falls too low on a lamp), finial washers (to ensure a tight finial fit), and shade clips (to allow fitter wires to work with glass reflector bowls).

A palette of plain and fancy papers for covering frames and rings. Be sure to use a low-watt bulb and/or spray the inside of your finished shade with a fire retardant to prevent burning.

THE LIGHT BULB

Before the light bulb, virtually all human activity ended at dusk. Most forms of lighting were messy, dangerous, and put out little light. In 1802, Humphrey Davy, an English chemist, passed an electric current through thin strips of metal, causing them to glow for a moment. Five years later and still experimenting with light, Davy used a strong battery to run a current through two carbon rods, producing an arc of electricity that leapt from one rod to the other and created a brilliant light. Arc lighting soon became popular, although its bright light could be used only in wide, open spaces and the fumes could be dangerous. Inventors continued to search for smaller, cheaper, and dimmer lighting that could be used in homes.

Enter Thomas Edison, a brilliant young misfit with a history of job drifting. With financial backing from J. Pierpont Morgan and a group of bankers, the Edison Electric Light Company was organized. Edison and his staff worked full time on lighting inventions. Edison had gone as far as inventing a glass bulb that could withstand the light's heat and keep outside air out, but he still needed a vacuum inside the bulb and a longer-burning material. It took Edison's workers more than 200 steps to make a single bulb. By accident, Edison discovered that a black residue, carbon, was itself a long-burning substance, and an English inventor's vacuum pump solved the air problem.

Edison's company spent their days fine-tuning the idea and working on mass-production plans. Among other things, Edison devised an insulating material that allowed wires to run underground. On March 31, 1880, Wabash, Indiana, became the first municipality in America to be lighted by electricity. Few people understood electricity at the time, and Edison had difficulty finding people to work for him. Wiring mistakes were frequent, causing many fires. Eventually, the kinks were worked out, and when Edison died in 1931, the suggestion to honor him by turning off the nation's electricity for 60 seconds was made. After much consideration, the idea was rejected.

decorative paper can be used, although many of them require a low-watt bulb and are not color-fast, so they'll need to be displayed in an area that does not receive direct sunlight. There are also heavier papers made specifically for lamp shade making.

A well-made lamp shade frame can last more than 50 years. In other words, if you see a stained, torn, and tattered shade at a garage sale or a flea market (or in your living room), grab it! Remove the outer shade material and sand off any remaining adhesive, then recover it.

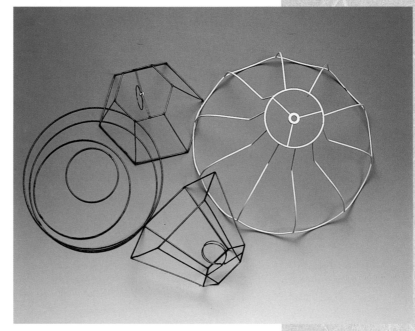

Metal shade frames and rings in a variety of shapes and sizes. The hardware on frames and fitter rings varies: some come with a clip that snaps over a light bulb, while others have a center fitting for use with a harp and finial.

MAKING CONE-SHAPED SHADES

Making a cone-shaped shade from scratch is a rewarding experience, especially if you don't rush through it. The first step is to purchase top and bottom rings.

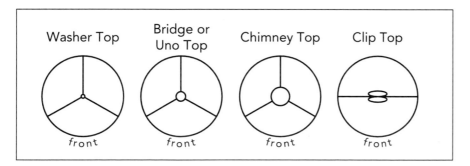

Most professional lamp shade crafters strongly advise you to choose the shade's base before you start the shade. Believe it or not, it's much harder to match a base to a shade than vice versa. Inspect the hardware of your base so you will

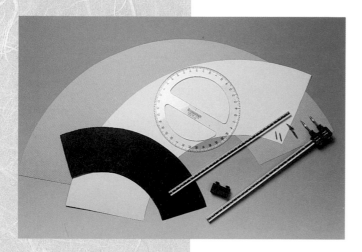

Constructing handmade shades is a simple, yet precise process. Measure carefully to ensure a well-fitting arc and invest in quality tools. Bulldog clips, a glue applicator bottle, and a small paintbrush speeds the assembly process.

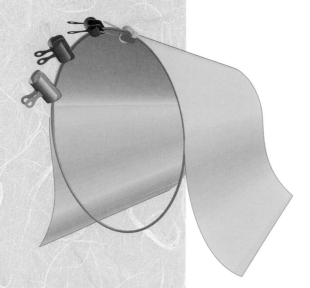

know what type of top fitter ring to purchase. Place your rings on a flat surface and make sure they rest flat; if not, gently bend them to straighten. Spray paint the rings with several coats of rust retardant if you live in a humid area.

Measure the diameter (the distance across a circle) of the top and bottom rings, and determine how tall you want your shade to be. (The height should complement the base as well as the area in which the shade will reside.) Use these three measurements to purchase a predrafted arc pattern. (Alternately, you can copy the arc pattern from an old lamp shade if the dimensions are the same.) A well-drafted arc pattern will fall perfectly onto the rings. If it doesn't, avoid the temptation to trim off excess material, which changes the dimensions and forms a lopsided shade.

Next, mark the center front of your arc pattern at the top and the bottom, and add a $^1/_2$" back seam allowance on the right edge. Place the arc pattern on the wrong side of your fabric or paper and add weights at both edges to prevent shifting. Trace the outline with a pencil, then mark the center and seam allowance $^1/_4$" into the shade material.

Hold the bottom wire ring with one hand in line with your body. Hold the arc at its bottom center front, right side up, with your other hand. Place the bottom center front of the arc on the wire ring and fasten the edge with a bulldog clip at a 45 degree angle. Working toward the left, continue fitting and fastening the arc to the ring until you reach the edge.

Return to the center front and fit the right half to the ring. When you reach the end, overlap the back seam left over right, and fasten with a bulldog clip. Look over your arc to make sure there are no gaps and that the arc's edge fits evenly around the edge. Stand the arc upright on a flat surface with its center front facing you.

Fit the top fitter wire ring just inside the top edge of the arc and secure with a bulldog clip at the center front. Fit the ring to the arc as you did the bottom, working first to the right and then to the left. Overlap the back seam right over left and secure with a bulldog clip. Check the top and bottom for a smooth, snug fit.

With the back seam facing you, lightly mark the top and bottom seam allowance. Remove all bulldog clips and set the rings aside. Place the arc on a flat work surface with its right side facing up. The pencil marks for the back seam overlap should be on your right. Occasionally, the back seam overlap will not be straight. Use a straight edge to connect the top and bottom markings and trim off any excess material.

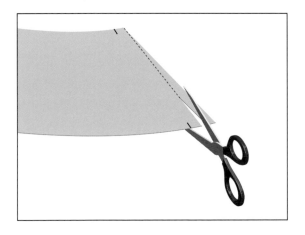

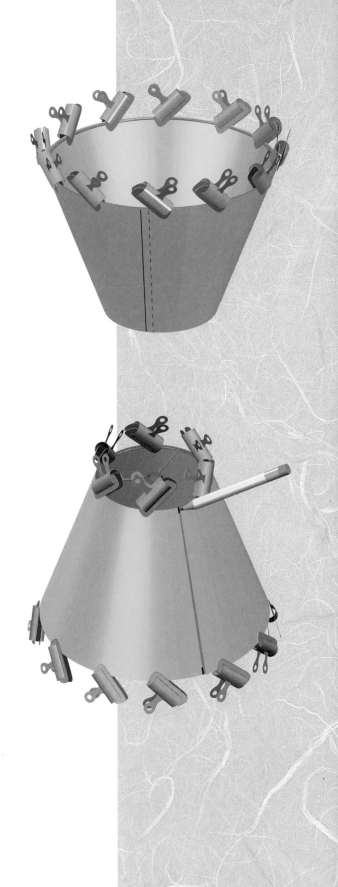

THE SCIENCE OF LIGHT

Defining light has been a challenge to the scientific community for hundreds of years. Before 1905, light was viewed as a wave, operating in a similar fashion to ocean waves. After 1905, however, scientists observed that light also behaved like particles, for example when light interacts with a small body, such as an atom or electron. Today's understanding of light involves an acceptance of both explanations.

The light visible to human eyes covers a wavelength range from about 400 nanometers (violet light) to 700 nanometers (red light). Yellow light falls in the center of this range, with a wavelength of about 500 nanometers. White light is actually a combination of several different wavelengths, and can be separated back into its component colors by bending the waves through a prism. When you look at a rainbow, you're seeing the effect of raindrops acting as prisms, bending sunlight of different wavelengths and spreading them out as color.

Human sight is very dependent on light. The outer parts of the eye, particularly the lens, focus their photons (packets of light energy) on the retina, a very thin, light-sensitive organ. The retina uses light-sensitive photoceptor cells—called cones and rods —to see images. (One human eye contains approximately three million cones and one million rods.) The retina uses cones in bright light, whereas rods, which cannot distinguish colors, are used in low light. This explains why you see only shades of gray on a moonlit night.

S H O P P I N G   T I P S

Making shades from scratch requires attention to detail when shopping for materials. Experts offer the following advice.

- If you're making a shade to fit a specific lamp, always bring the lamp with you.
- Know what type of fitter wire you will use to attach the shade to the lamp. (clip top, clip-on bulb, washer top, chimney top, etc.)
- Hold potential fabrics or papers up to the light before making a final decision. Some materials, woven fabrics especially, can be deceiving.
- Choose a construction technique before you go shopping. Write the formulas for calculating material amounts on an index card, and bring along a small calculator and tape measure. When in doubt, purchase extra.
- If mail-ordering, avoid the temptation to discuss color over the phone. Request or purchase samples.

Turn the arc over so that its wrong side faces up. Remove any excess pencil markings with an art gum eraser. Apply a thin, even coat of glue along the entire length of the back seam overlap. Lift the left edge of the arc and hold it so that the right side is facing you, and apply a thin, even coat of glue along the back seam allowance on the right side, bringing the glue out to the edge.

Line up the top right hand edge of the arc with the left side's pencil mark and fasten with a bulldog clip placed parallel to the arc's edge. Secure the bottom in the same way. Hold the glued seam lines together with two hands.

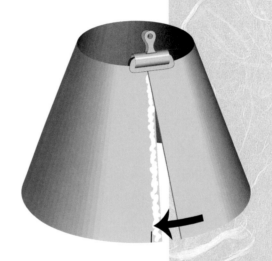

Place the arc seam side down on waxed paper and remove the bulldog clips. Clean off any excess glue with a clean cloth, then place weights along the back seam. Remove the weights when the glue is dry.

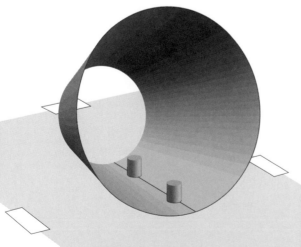

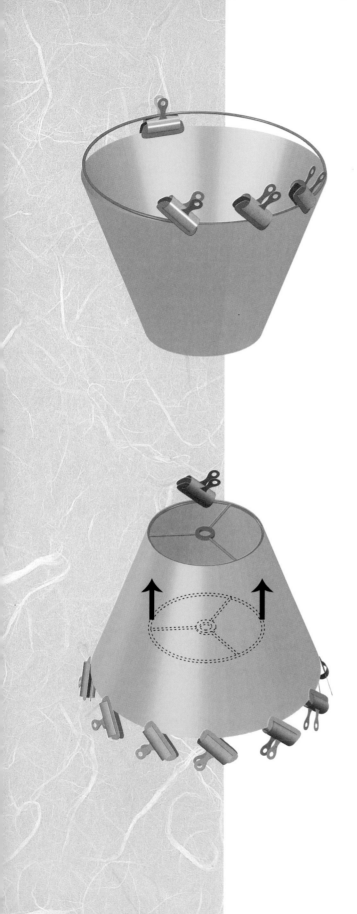

Apply a thin line of glue around the arc's inside edge, rotating the arc as you work. Place one bulldog clip at the back seam, parallel to the arc's edge, avoiding glue contact. Turn the arc so that the back seam is away from you. Ease the bottom wire ring to the inside edge at the center front and fasten with a bulldog clip at a 45-degree angle. Repeat with three or four clips on both sides of the first clip. Lift the ring from the back clip and ease the ring into place. Fasten with clips as you did for the front.

Turn the arc upright and apply glue to the top inside edge. Slip the top fitter wire ring up through the bottom with one hand and carefully pull it in place from the top with your other hand so that the fitter wire is recessed into the arc. Fasten at the center front with a bulldog clip. Adjust the ring to fit evenly with the arc's top edge and secure with clips. Allow at least one hour to dry, then remove clips.

The next step is to finish the top and bottom edges with some sort of decorative trim. Five-eights-inch grosgrain ribbon is the most popular binding, although colored tapes, velvets, and twills can also be used. Avoid polyester trims — they stretch and do not bond well with glue. To determine the amount of binding you will need, multiply the top and bottom ring diameters by four and add them together.

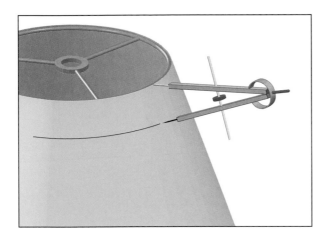

Draw a guideline (preferably with a drafting compass) around the top and bottom edges. When working on the bottom edge, it helps to allow a portion of the shade to hang over the edge. Square off one end of the binding for the top of the shade. Apply glue to the lower half of the first few inches, starting at the squared off end. Working from the

back seam, position the binding ¼" to the left of the seam overlap. (The bottom edge of the ribbon should just cover the guide line.) Fingerpress the trim into place and allow a minute or so for the glue to set.

Working in 10" increments, apply glue to the lower half of the binding, taking care to hold the binding away from the shade. Position and fingerpress the binding as you did before. Repeat until you reach the back seam, then cut away any excess binding perpendicular to the shade's edge. Allow at least ten minutes for the glue to dry. Cut neat, v-shaped slashes in the binding for ease at all points where fitter wires connect to ring wires.

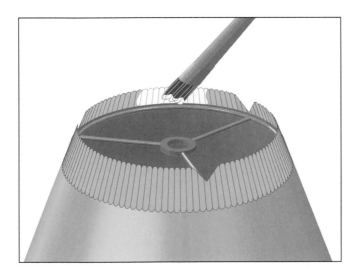

Apply a thin, even coat of glue to the inside of the remaining ribbon. Roll and mold the binding over the top of the wire, taking extra care for a smooth fit around the fitter wires. Crease the edge of the binding snugly and remove any excess glue. Repeat the process for the bottom edge, omitting the slashes since there are no bottom fitter wires.

Making Multipaneled Shades

Multipaneled shade frames come in a fascinating variety of shapes, from contemporary hexagons to scalloped Tiffanys. One look through a supplier's catalog will leave your imagination brimming with project ideas. To cover a multipaneled frame with paper, simply turn the frame on its side on top of the paper's wrong side and trace the outline. Rotate the frame as you work until you return to the starting point. Add a $1/2$" folding allowance to the edges and at the side seam.

Cut out the paper, then center it over the frame. Glue one side edge of the paper to a strut, then brush a light layer of white craft glue over the top folding allowance. Roll the paper down over the top frame wire and glue in place. Repeat with the bottom edge, then glue the back seam in place. If the paper isn't taut enough or if it loosens as time passes, place the shade in front of a small space heater for 20 minutes.

Covering a multipaneled shade frame with a lining or outer fabric is a little more challenging since most glues are uncooperative. First, trace each panel onto plain white paper. Add a 1" seam allowance on all sides and cut out the patterns from your fabric and your chosen backing material on the bias. Label the pattern pieces A, B, C, etc, and label the matching panels the same way with masking tape. (Even if all the panels look exactly alike, they're sometimes slightly different. Skip this step at your own risk.)

Tightly wrap all wire areas at an angle with bias tape in a compatible color, securing as needed with small stitches. Attach the backing material (styrene or fusible interfacing) to the fabric pieces. Working with one panel at a time, stretch the fabric over the panel and pin in place over the top and bottom wires.

Slip-stitch the top edge of the fabric to the bias tape, restretch the fabric, and repeat at the bottom edge. Each additional panel piece will need to have its side seam pressed down and slip-stitched over the preceding section. Attach ribbon, cording, or other decorative trims to cover the side seams.

PAIRING SHADES AND BASES

Choosing the perfect shade for a base—or choosing the perfect base for a shade—can be more challenging than you'd guess. If your shade brims with bright color and pattern, you should probably play it safe and choose something less competing for the base. Also give some thought to combining shades and bases with complementary proportions, as outlined below.

Cone-shape shades tend to look best with bases that are wider and heavier at the bottom.

Hexagon shades flatter Early American-style bases.

Empire shades look great with vases and Early American-style bases.

Bell-shaped shades look nice on vase- and urn-style bases.

Drum shapes work well on column lamps and bases that are heavier at the bottom.

Oval shades look nice with bases with oval lines.

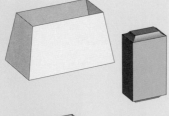

Square and rectangular shades work well with square and almost-square bases.

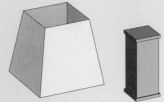

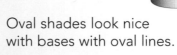

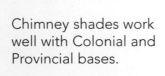

Chimney shades work well with Colonial and Provincial bases.

DECORATIVE PAPER SHADES

Made from decorative, marbled papers, these cone-shaped shades were formed around rings recycled from old shades. To make a cone shade, roll a sheet of decorative paper into a cone shape with similar diameters to the rings. Secure the seam with two coats of rubber cement.

Stand the cone upside down in a wastebasket. Coat the top ring with white glue and set it as far down in the cone as it will go, taking care to keep it aligned with the cone's axis. (Otherwise your bulb may touch the shade.) Leave the ring to dry, then repeat the process with the larger bottom ring. Cut off any excess paper. Finish with decorative trims and/or cut patterns into the lower edge if desired.

DESIGN: PAT SCHEIBLE
MARBLED PAPERS: PATTY SCHLEICHER, MIMI SCHLEICHER

COLLAGED SHADES

Simple collage techniques are a great way to recycle plain or dingy shades. For a translucent effect, use a thin, fibrous paper shade. Matching finials make a nice touch.

To make the shades, cut or tear small pieces from an interesting selection of gift wrap papers, fabrics, and threads. Coat the backs of the pieces with a thin coat of brush-on acrylic medium (gloss or matte finish) and smooth them in place. Continue adding layers until you are pleased with the effect. Allow the acrylic medium to dry completely, then apply a finish coat of watered-down polymer medium. Note: A light coat of watercolor paints can help blend disparate sections

DESIGN: SANDY WEBSTER

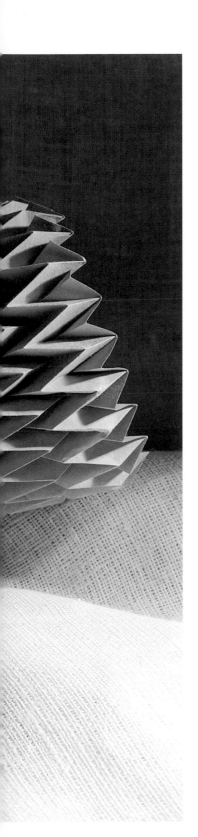

ORIGAMI SHADES

Origami, the ancient Japanese art of paper folding, can be adapted for use with lamp shades, creating beautiful lighting effects. These shades were all made on the reverse fold with the same basic techniques; the finishing techniques create their distinct designs. Interesting variations of these shades can be created by experimenting with different fold widths and diagonal line angles.

If you're new to reverse fold origami, making one or more practice samples is very helpful. Fan fold a piece of typing paper lengthwise four times to make four sections of paper with three fan folds or reverse folds. With the reverse folds closed, fold up one corner diagonally, then fold down the end opposite the corner just folded at a 45 degree angle. For practice, the distance between point A and point B is not important, just be

DESIGN: KATHY OLER

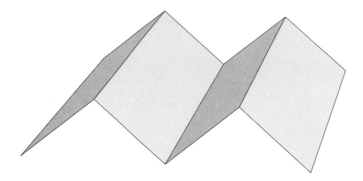

sure to place the fold close enough to allow for at least two more folds before you run out of paper.

As with the corner fold, refold this fold along the same crease to the back. Now fold in the same way at least two or three more times so that there are at least four diagonal crease lines along the

length of folded paper. Carefully unfold the paper. A herringbone pattern of faint crease lines should be apparent.

Starting at one end, gently crease the first row of diagonal creases so that all of the folds are in the same direction. (This is like the first row of a fan fold except that the fold will be along the diagonal lines rather than a straight line.) After creasing the first row in the same direction, move to the second row and crease these diagonal folds in the opposite direction. Continue this preliminary creasing until all of the diagonal creases in the same row are folded in the same direction, with each row of diagonal

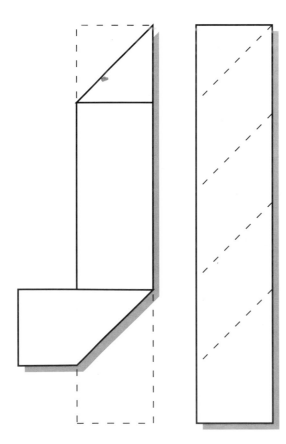

creases folding in the opposite or reverse direction.

At this point the paper should almost collapse into the complicated folding pattern. If it does not easily collapse, go back along each individual row of diagonal creases and flatten each fold, making a sharper fold along the crease line. The collapsed paper should look like the illustration from the side. Practice this folding process several times.

To begin making a shade, determine the size of paper you will need by measuring the diameter of the bottom of your shade frame and the distance from top to bottom. Choose a 50 or 60 pound kraft paper or a gift wrap that can withstand multiple foldings. Paper that is too soft or too brittle will not hold the folds or willl tear. Solid paper colors create the best highlights, allowing the light to define shape and surface.

Multiply the diameter of the bottom ring by 3.14 (pi). Multiply your answer by 2.75, and cut the length of your paper to this measurement. It's important that the length of the paper be an odd number of inches to successful seam matching, so add an inch if you come up with an even answer. (With experience, you can reduce the factor to 2.5.) Multiply the height of your shade frame by 2 (can later be reduced to 1.5) and use your answer to determine the width of your paper. Cut out the paper to these measurements. (If necessary, you can glue lengths of paper together with $1/2$" overlapping seams.) Prepare the frame by wrapping the rings and side struts with gummed paper tape cut in narrow widths.

Using a T-square and a pencil, lightly mark off 1" fold lines for the first set of reverse (fan) folds on the wrong side of the paper. Score the fold lines on the wrong side with a bone folder or other appropriate tool and a straight edge. Mark the diagonal fold lines with a pencil and a straight edge. Notice how the diagonal fold lines are mirror images across a vertical fold line. Place the straight edge along the diagonal from one corner of the paper to the bottom of the vertical fold line that is the same distance from the corner as the paper is wide. Mark diagonal lines along the straight edge in alternating folds. Remember that the diagonal folds alternate in mirror images across vertical fold lines, so one line drawn from the corner of the paper to the bottom along the straight edge will create fold lines traveling in the wrong direction.

Move the straight edge over to the next 1" mark and repeat. Continue marking all of the diagonal in one direction, then mark the diagonals in the other direction, starting in the top right corner. Score the diagonal fold lines on the wrong side. (Avoid any temptation to skip the marking and measuring steps.)

After all of the fold lines have been marked and scored, proceed with creasing and folding. In the practice directions, all of the fold lines were creased in the correct direction prior to collapsing the folds; now it may be easier to work with one row of the diagonal folds at a time because the paper is much larger. Begin by gently creasing the diagonal fold lines along the first row in one direction so right side of the paper folds toward the back. (This fold is often referred to a hill fold because it forms a fold that appears to stand up from the right side. Once all the fold lines have been creased, repress them again to make them sharper. If the folds have been correctly made, the top edge of the paper will look as if furrows have been folded into it. The vertical fold in the middle of the triangular furrow folded toward the back is now a valley fold, appearing to sink away from the paper's right side.

Collapse the paper, making sure that all of the folds are aligned in the correct direction. Press the newly made folds together to ensure a tight fold. Your collapsed paper should look like the illustration from the side. Turn the paper over so that the wrong side faces up. Crease the next row of diagonal folds, again forming hill folds. (Note: When the paper is turned to the right side again, these hill folds will be valley folds from the front.) As these diagonal folds are creased, the vertical folds need to be reversed. It may be easier at this point to gently reverse one or two of the vertical folds at a time and then crease the corresponding diagonal folds. Once the diagonal folds for the second row are creased, go back and make the diagonal folds sharper. Keeping the folds gathered as you work helps keep all the folds in the correct direction. Firm the folds once the row has been completed by collapsing the paper and pressing.

Repeat the above procedure for each of the remaining rows of diagonal folds, flipping the paper from right to wrong side and vice versa, initially creasing the diagonal folds into hill or valley folds and reversing the vertical folds, and, finally, collapsing the paper and pressing all of the folds together. Make sure that the vertical lines at the top and the bottom edges do not split, especially the first and last rows of diagonal folds.

After you've finished folding, join the ends by carefully bringing the two short ends of the paper together with their right sides facing out to form a cylinder. Clip the edges, being careful not to mar the paper's surface. Place the cylinder over the wire frame. It may be helpful to elevate the frame so that the cylinder can fit down over the wire frame in its eventual position. Using one or more strips of paper, ribbon, or fabric, circle the cylinder at the places where it will be attached to the wire frame and draw up the strips until the inner folds make contact with the wire. Loosely secure the strips to hold the folds. Adjust the folds evenly around the frame. If you need more folds, mark the vertical fold line that can be used as a cutting line for reducing the cylinder's size. Remove the shade, cut to size, and refit. When the shade fits the frame satisfactorily, release the strips and the clips.

If folds must be cut off, make sure to end up with an odd number of vertical folds so that the two folds, which overlap for the seam, match, similar to matching plaids in fabric. Glue the seam by applying rubber cement to the right side of one fold and to the wrong side of the opposite side.

After the rubber cement has completely dried, use the strips again to refit the shade to the frame. Space the folds evenly around the frame. Brush on a small amount of a clear-drying, tacky glue at the contact points. Let the glue dry, then repeat with a second application. Ideally, you want to use just enough glue to hold the shade in place without using so much that it crinkles or distorts the paper.

For the cone-shaped shades, fold the paper and join it in a cylinder as described above. String the row of folds on heavy thread with a sharp needle, poking through the uppermost point created at the top of 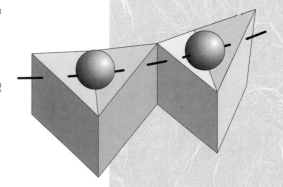 the shade by the folds, piercing all four layers of paper at each point. Gather the thread to fit the frame. (Note: For further embellishment, beads can be strung on the thread and positioned between the folds.)

CUT AND PIERCED SHADES

Cut and pierced paper shades have a sculpted, three-dimensional appeal to them during daylight, and their designs create interesting variations in light shading during evening hours.

To make a cut and pierced shade, transfer your pattern to the back side of your arc with a light pencil. Prepare a work surface by folding a terry cloth towel in half and placing the arc on top of it with its right side facing down. Begin following the pattern with a piercer, using the smaller needle for accent holes and the larger needle for main designs. (Piercers can be found in larger craft supply stores; they usually have two needles and resemble an ice pick.) The needle should easily bounce out from the paper, creating an attractive, candlewicked appearance on the right side of the paper.

After all of the piercing is finished, tape the edges of a 9 x 12 sheet of framing glass and place the arc on the glass with its right side facing down. Begin the cutwork with a

DESIGN: CHRIS NOAH-COOPER

31

craft knife and a fine, sharp blade. The goal is to make even cuts without jerking. (Note: Beginners often use too much pressure, which breaks off the blade tips, so wear some form of eye protection.) Be sure to leave at least $1/16$" between cuts and to fix any tears with a small amount of clear-drying craft glue.

For shades also incorporating painted scenes or patterns, take extra care to avoid getting large areas of paper wet and to avoid using too much water on any specific area to prevent permanent buckling and destruction of the paper's top surface. Keep in mind that mistakes such as splattered paint that can be satisfactorily fixed on the outer side of the shade will show from the inside when the bulb is lit.

To finish the shade, gently erase all pencil marks, then attach the arc to a frame and add desired trims as directed in the basic instructions on pages 12 - 18.

See page 113 for cutout and stenciling patterns.

LEAF LAMPSHADE

The six sections in a hexagon shade frame create great potential for surface designing. To make this shade, measure and cut out shapes from heavy artist's paper to fit the sections. Search out an interesting variety of leaves, then make stencils from them. Paint the shapes with an ultra sheer layer of artist's oil paint, arranging them to overlap as desired. See page 112 for leaf pattern.

DESIGN: PAT SCHEIBLE

Classic Cube Shade

This simple cube shade is assembled from wood dowels and squares of rice paper, and is then placed over a self-standing socket. Try using colored bulbs for special occasions.

To make the shade, cut $1/4$" wood dowels exactly 8" in length. Make a flat square from four of the dowels, arranging them in windmill fashion, and secure them with hot glue. Repeat to make a second flat square. Sand or scrape any glue bubbles off the surface.

Attach one dowel length to each corner and secure with hot glue. Each dowel should be standing at a 90-degree angle to the bottom piece. Position the second square against these dowels and hot-glue it in place one corner at a time. Sand off any glue globs.

Smooth an even layer of glue around one side of the cube. Line up one corner of the paper with one of the cube's corners and smooth the paper into the glue. Trim the remaining two edges of the paper with a craft knife and a ruler. Repeat on the remaining sides. Use with a low-watt bulb.

DESIGN: ANN YANCY

GIFT PAPER SHADE

Decorative gift papers come in a wonderful assortment of colorful patterns and are simple to attach to shade frames. To make a shade, measure and cut out pieces of paper approximately 2" larger on all sides than each section of a multipaneled shade frame. Apply a thin bead of white craft glue to one panel of the frame.

Hold a piece of paper over the panel and play with positioning. Carefully lay the paper in place a little at a time, smoothing as you go. If the paper is mis-laid, throw it away and begin again. After the glue has set (at least 20 minutes), use small, sharp scissors to neatly trim away the excess paper, taking care not to lift the paper up from the frame. Continue with the next panel until you've finished. Avoid the temptation to glue more than one panel at a time. Apply decorative trims as desired.

DESIGN: LEAH NALL

HANDMADE PAPER SHADES

Handmade papers (found in most art supply stores) are simple to fit around shade frames, providing a pleasant look during the day and additional intrigue at night when the bulb light reveals the natural beauty of pulp fibers. When choosing a frame, look for an unusual shape to complement the uniqueness of the paper.

To make the shade, place a frame on the wrong side of a sheet of paper. Trace the frame's shape onto the paper, rotating the frame as you work. Add a $1/2$" allowance on all sides and cut out the paper.

With a course, brittle brush, stroke on a light coat of white craft glue $1/2$" in on the wrong side of one edge. Roll the paper around one of the side struts, leaving $1/2$" of excess paper at the top and bottom. Coat the top and bottom edges with glue and roll them around the frame, making short cuts in the paper edge if needed for ease around corners. Glue the last edge against the paper.

Additional detailing can be added by gluing decorative motifs to the outside of the paper. Motifs cut from contrasting paper colors can be enjoyed all of the time, whereas motifs cut from the same paper as the shade can be seen only when the bulb is illuminated at night. For an added touch, consider covering the side seam with decorative stitching using a tapestry needle and a natural fiber such as raffia. See page 110 for fish patterns.

DESIGN: JONATHAN P. STUCKY, OPPOSITE PAGE, LEFT AND ABOVE
DESIGN: KIM TIBBALS, OPPOSITE PAGE, RIGHT

TOPOGRAPHICAL MAP SHADE

Here's a fun way to make use of colorful vacation maps. Begin by ironing the wrong side of the map on a nonsteam setting. Trace the shape of a multipaneled wire frame onto the wrong side of the map, rotating the frame as you work. Add ¹/₂" folding allowance to all sides and cut out.

Center the frame from top to bottom over the map and glue one side edge to the frame. Fold the top and bottom edges over the frame and glue in place. Glue the last side edge in place when you're back to the starting point. Cover the edges and side struts with a bright color of narrow masking tape.

DESIGN: PAT SCHEIBEL

PARTY SHADES

These colorful shades are a quick, spontaneous way to change your everyday lighting for a special occasion. To make a shade, cut out a large triangle or rectangle from hardware cloth or chicken wire. Experiment with different folds and bends in the wire until you're happy with the overall shape.

Spray a small surface area with an aerosol adhesive, then press interesting shapes torn or cut from handmade or tissue papers into the adhesive, allowing the shapes to overlap in some areas. Place the shade in front of a light source, then add additional scraps of paper if desired.

DESIGN: OLIVIER ROLLIN

WINDOW SHADES

Embellishing a simple paper shade with window cuts and decorative shapes creates two distinctive looking shades. When viewed in the daytime, the windows and paper shapes look like playful embellishment. In the evening, the windows and shapes become part of the shade, casting interesting shadows and colored light, and creating new colors. Geometric frames with built-in sections provide predetermined sections for working.

Begin by placing a frame on the wrong side of a sheet of paper. (The visible strands of pulp in handmade papers add interest, especially when the shade is illuminated, but many of the brilliantly colored papers are not colorfast and will need to be kept out of direct sunlight to prevent fading.)

Trace the shape onto the paper and rotate the frame to the next section. Continue tracing and rotating until you've traced the entire frame. Add an extra ½" allowance on all sides and cut out the paper. Place the frame on top of the paper's wrong side ½" away from a vertical strut and centered top to bottom. Using a coarse, brittle brush, apply a light coat of glue on the side ½" and roll the paper around the strut. Coat the protruding top and bottom ½" with glue and roll them around the frame.

Place the papered shade in front of a small heat source (a portable heater) to absorb the paper's excess moisture and pull the paper tight against the frame. After the glue has completely dried, cut windows into the paper with a craft knife. (Tip: Change the blade in your craft knife as soon as it becomes slightly dull to prevent tearing the paper.) Do not open the windows yet.

Cut out interesting shapes from additional paper and glue them in place. Note: You may want to hold the proposed paper shapes against the shade when it's illuminated to see if you like the color changes. Open the windows. See pages 108 and 109 for geometric patterns and shapes.

DESIGN: JONATHAN P. STUCKY

Victorian Shades

Many of the qualities associated with the Victorian era—extravagant detailing, lush colors, and fine handwork—can be seen in these exquisite shades. Silk velvets and chiffons are good fabric choices for these shades.

To make the angel shade, line and cover a multi-paneled frame as directed above, using an angel print fabric for the center panel. Do not add the trim yet. To create a sugared effect over the angel, spray on an even layer of acrylic adhesive. Sprinkle miniature glass beads over the panel and gently press them in place. After the acrylic dries, finish with a coat of clear sealer, then trim as desired.

To make the pink shade, lower left, line a metal frame and cover the plain panels as directed above.

The side fabric panels in this shade have been ruched, a type of gathering that creates soft, informal pleating and is especially attractive on narrow areas. To make a ruched panel, cut the fabric slightly wider than the panel and about twice as high. Stitch several rows of gathering stitches on the long edges. Pull the gathers and sew in place. Trim off any excess fabric, then finish with decorative trim as desired.

To make the large shade shown below, line a multi-paneled metal shade frame, referring to the basic instructions on page 18 if necessary. Determine which panels will be plain and which will have open fan pleats. For the plain panels, cut the fabric on the straight of grain slightly larger than the panel. Pin the fabric to the lining, stretching

DESIGN: MARY MAXWELL

for a tight fit, and hand stitch in place. Trim off any excess fabric, taking extra care not to cut the lining.

For the open fan pleated sections, cut out the chiffon slightly larger in height and twice the panel's width. Stitch two rows of gathering stitches on the short bottom edge. Pull the gathers until the width is slightly larger than the panel. Adjust all of the gathers to the center of the panel, leaving some ungathered fabric on both sides. Pin into place

and stitch down as you did for the plain panels. Pull the pleats into position, starting at the center and working from side to side until all of the bottom panel is pleated. Reinforce the pleated chiffon with additional hand stitching.

Cover the side seams by attaching a decorative silk trim with fabric glue. Glue a length of fringe to the bottom edges, adding tassels at the side struts if desired, then finish with a row of trim at the top and bottom edges.

LAMP SHADE CHROMATOGRAPHY

Chromatography is a simple way to create spontaneous color combinations on a fabric lamp shade. Find
a fabric shade that has not been laminated or stiffened.
Fill your bathtub with ³/₈" of water. Drip liquid
watercolors around the rim, then carefully set the
shade into the water. Don't worry if some of the color
flows off the shade. Loosely drape a plastic bag
around the shade to keep the air humid. Remove the
shade after several hours. Blot the rim on newspaper,
then dry it with a hair dryer.

DESIGN: PAT SCHEIBLE

Faux Marbled Shade

Faux marbling is a simple way to transform inexpensive fabric shades into custom creations. Start with a fabric shade in a dark, solid color. Soak a wide artist's brush in water, then dip an edge into white acrylic paint. Start painting at the top and work down at an angle. Vary the amount of color you apply as much as possible—just a wash in some areas while quite heavy in others. Allow the base color occasionally to show through and keep your brush wet for maximum control. When the paint has completely dried, add designs that look like lightning streaks with a metallic paint pen and puff fabric paint.

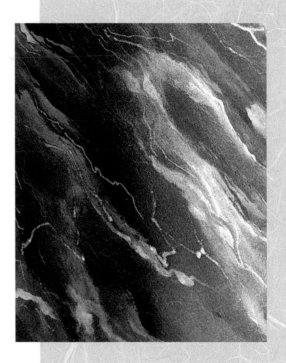

DESIGN: MARY JANE MILLER

PAINTED SILK SHADES

The popularity of painting on silk continues to increase as crafters lose their intimidation of this simple art form. If you're new to silk painting, it's well worth your time to review several books on materials and techniques.

Begin with a metal shade frame covered in white silk. Draw the outlines of your designs on the silk with resist. (Resist is a wax-like substance that contains the paint in a certain area.) Paint in the dye, then steam-set the color. Finish by washing out the resist. Avoid displaying the shade in direct sunlight to prevent the colors from fading.

Note: If you love the look of painted silk but don't feel comfortable with your drawing skills, you can place a pattern behind the silk and trace it with the resist.

DESIGN: ANN SILBERLICHT

SILK EMBROIDERED SHADE

Silk cording can be used in any number of creative ways to add simple styling to an ordinary shade. To make the shade, measure and mark off $^1/_2$" intervals on the bottom, top, and side edges with a disappearing fabric pen. Measure and mark off needle holes about 1" up from the center bottom of each panel for the v-shape design. Punch holes through the marks with a tapestry needle.

Wrap a short length of masking tape around one end of the silk cording to form a protective, firm covering. (The cording will unravel if you use the needle.) Work the cording through the holes from front to back, taking care to hide the knots in the corners on the wrong side.

DESIGN: KIM TIBBALS

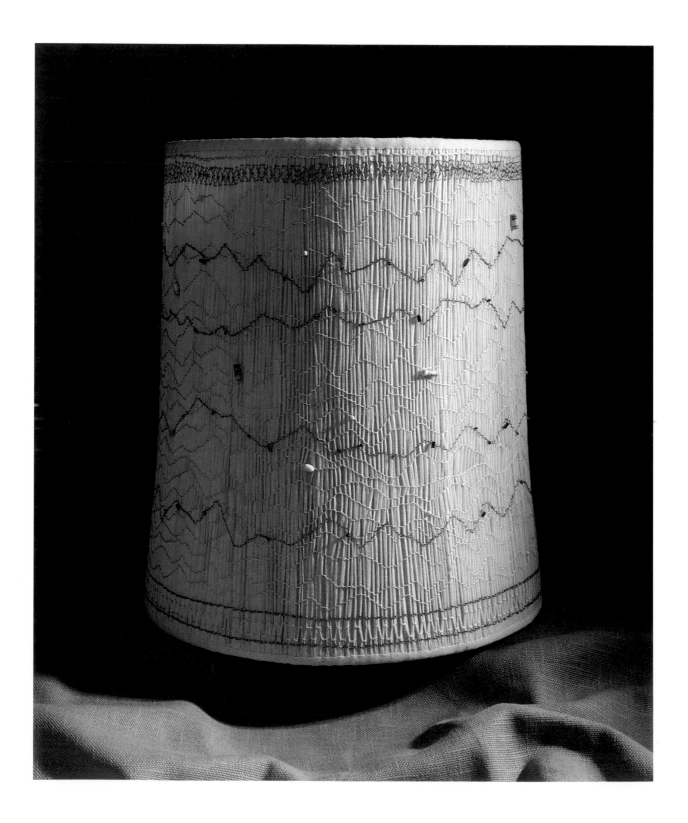

SMOCKED SHADE

The soft pleats in smocking make a lovely fabric to diffuse light. To make the shade, choose a sheer, all-cotton gauze that's four to five times as wide as your shade frame's circumference. Measure the height of your frame and add 2", then cut out the fabric to these dimensions, piecing if necessary.

Sew the short edges together with right sides facing to form a tube. Divide the tube into as many sections as there are side struts and mark these points top and bottom to help arrange the gathers evenly. Lay the top of the tube on a gridded cutting board with the fabric's grain lined up with the grid. Mark four rows of vertical dots in $1/2$" increments at the top and bottom. (If the shade is especially large or you're new to smocking, an extra two rows of dots around the middle can be helpful for aligning the pleats.)

Thread a needle with a length of buttonhole twist or topstitching thread that's long enough to go all the way around the fabric plus a foot. Working on the wrong side, pick up the dots and carefully gather two rows at a time to tightly fit the frame. Smock in the stitches of your choices with a pearl cotton and a fine metallic braid, adding beads if desired, with at least two sturdy rows at the top and the bottom.

Fold the top and bottom edges over the frame and stitch tightly to the bias tape wraps. Fit a lining to the wrong side, sewing it in place very tightly and covering all raw edges. Cut a strip of fabric on the bias about four times the circumference of the shade for the top and the bottom. Press narrow hems under, then fold them over the rims and hand stitch tightly in place to form a lining

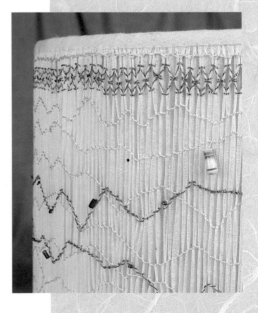

DESIGN: CAROL PARKS

SLIPCOVER SHADES

These colorful slipcover shades slide over a plain shade to add instant color and pizazz to any room. To make the beaded shade, first make a pattern by rolling a shade on paper, tracing the edges as you roll. Add a back seam allowance, then cut out one from your fabric, one from fusible knit, and one from fusing film.

Fuse the knit to the back of the fabric, then fuse the film to the knit. Glue or stitch some silver cording in place, then glue the pearl strings in place. Reinforce the hanging pearls by stitching them at their points. Glue the back seam allowance.

To make the necktie shade, make a pattern as you did for the beaded shade. Cut out one piece of fusible knit and one piece of fusing film from the pattern. Measure the bottom curves of the pattern and divide it into increments suitable for a tie shape. For example, if the base curve measures 25" you can make 10 ties with bottom widths of 2.5" each. Divide the top measurement by the number of ties you've planned and center the first increment over the base increment. The point of the tie is a right angle corner centered in the increment. Trace a pattern of the tie shape, adding a $^3/_8$" seam allowance to the sides, top, and point.

Cut out separate ties and decorate them with ribbon strips. Sew the ties together at their sides. Fuse the knit fabric to the back of the tie fabric, then fuse the film to the back of the knit fabric. Finish by gluing on a decorative edging of grosgrain ribbon at the top.

DESIGN: CAROLYN PIEPER–BENFORADO

CUSTOM FABRIC SHADES

Styrene backing and fusible interfacings allow you to custom design a shade that's perfect for any room, any style, any personality. Attention to detail creates a professional, polished look, so don't settle for less than the perfect fabric and trim.

To make one of the shades shown here, make a fabric shade as directed on page 18, adding appliqued shapes if desired before attaching the arc to the frame. Trim with imaginative colors and textures, braiding several colors together if needed to create the right look. For additional flair, string painted wood cutouts onto raffia or embroidery floss and thread through the top of the shade.

DESIGN: LEAH NALL, OPPOSITE PAGE
DESIGN: FRED GAYLOR, ABOVE

GATHERED FABRIC SHADE

If you don't have the patience (or time) to custom-fit a shade frame, consider this attractive alternative. Choose a crisp, non-wrinkle fabric for best results. Cut a rectangle of fabric that is the height of the frame plus 4" and twice the distance around the widest part of the frame. Sew the two short edges together with right sides facing. Press under $1/4$" on each long edge, and again 1". Stitch two or three rows of gathering stitches $1/8$" apart beginning $3/4$" in from the outer fold. Thread a length of cording through the folded edges. Place the fabric tube over the frame and pull the cording until the fabric fits the frame. Knot the excess cording and trim off any excess. Distribute the gathers evenly to finish.

SHADE & FABRIC DESIGN: DIANE GRINNELL

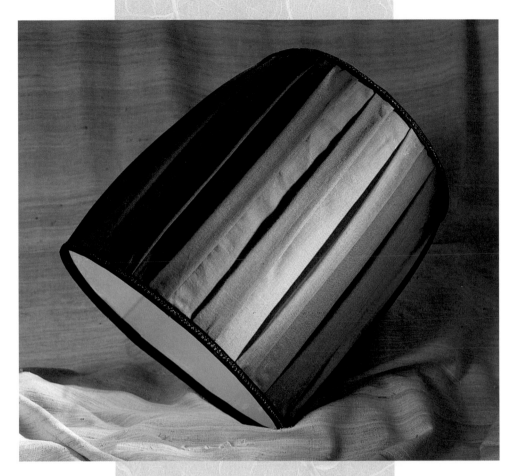

Box-Pleated Shade

Simple box pleats can add texture and color to an old drum-shaped shade. To make the shade, measure the height of your shade and add 1" to this measurement. Cut out a single piece of fabric to this height plus three times the circumference. Play with different widths and depths of pleats until you're happy with the look. Form box pleats around the top of the shade and secure each pleat against the rim with two clothes pins. Gently glue the top $^1/_2$" of pleated fabric to the rim, removing the clothespins as you work on a pleat and then reapplying them when you're finished. Repeat the process on the bottom edge, taking care to keep the pleats straight and vertical. Remove the clothes pins when the glue has dried and wipe off any excess glue with a damp cloth. Finish the top and bottom edges with bias tape and/or trim.

DESIGN: FRED GAYLOR

PLEATED SHADE

Paneled frames of all shapes and sizes offer crafters a versatile work space to showcase interesting fabric folds and pleats. To make this shade, line a metal shade frame, referring to the basic instructions on page 18 if necessary. Determine which panels will be plain and which will be pleated.

For the plain sections, cut out the fabric on the straight of grain slightly larger than one panel. Pin the fabric to the lining, stretching for a tight fit, and hand stitch in place. Carefully trim off any excess fabric, taking extra care not to cut the lining.

For the pleated sections, cut the fabric a little longer than the width and $2\frac{1}{2}$ to 3 times the panel's height. Mark the long side with evenly spaced pins or dots to help you line up the pleats. (Note: Adjust the width of your pleats to suit your fabric and the height of your frame.)

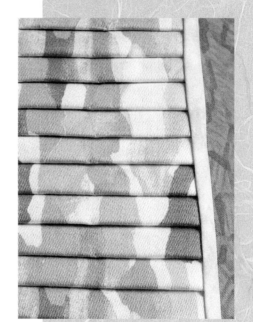

DESIGN: LEAH NALL

Fabric Origami Shade

The fine, sculptural quality of paper origami can also be created with stiffened fabric. Refer to a well-illustrated, basic origami book for extra folding practice if necessary.

To begin, cut out a 24" square of paper for folding practice and to test the fit. Fold the square in half diagonally to form a triangle, then fold in half again to form a smaller triangle. Open the triangle and press it into a square. Turn it over and repeat with the other side. Keeping the open edges on top, fold the outer edges in as shown and repeat on the other side.

Fold down the edges once again on each side to create a diamond-shaped form. Open the upper triangle and press the flaps down, then repeat on the other side. Fold the flaps inward on each side, then shape the origami with your fingers from the inside.

To prepare the fabric, iron a layer of fusible vinyl to its paper liner, referring to the manufacturer's instructions. Turn the paper liner over and place a piece of iridescent lamé on top of it, then place a piece of laminated polyester chiffon on top of the lamé. Carefully turn your fabric "sandwich" over and iron the vinyl until it fuses all three layers together.

Cut out a fabric square to your predetermined measurement. Fold the stiffened fabric as you did the paper. When you finish folding and shaping, sew each of the flaps in place with a special button and machine-stitch the edges.

DESIGN: CAROLYN PIEPER-BENFORADO

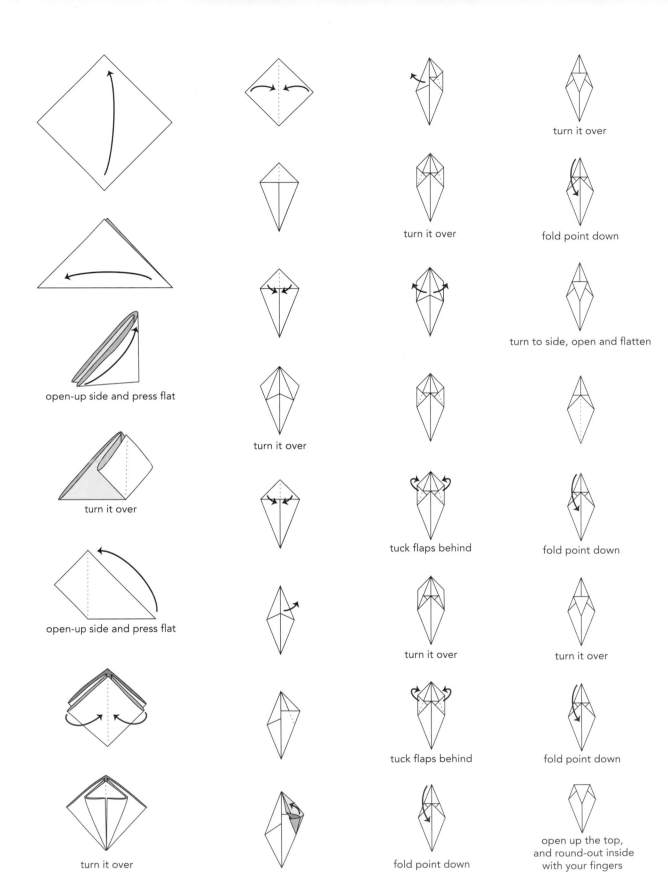

turn it over

fold point down

turn to side, open and flatten

open-up side and press flat

turn it over

tuck flaps behind

fold point down

turn it over

open-up side and press flat

turn it over

turn it over

turn it over

tuck flaps behind

fold point down

turn it over

fold point down

open up the top,
and round-out inside
with your fingers

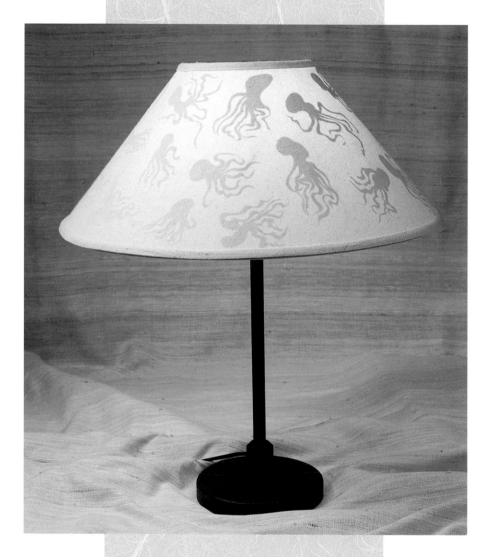

OCTOPI SHADE

One of the great wonders of lamp shade lighting involves interior motifs. Designs applied to the inside of your shade will not show through during the day. When you light the bulb at night, though, the motifs suddenly appear, brilliant and magical. To make this shade, trace the motif of your choice onto the back side of adhesive kitchen drawer contact paper. Cut out the shapes, then paint the patterned side in the same color as the interior of the shade. Peel off the backing layer and stick the motifs in place inside the shade.

See octopi patterns on page 112.

DESIGN: MARY JANE MILLER

Spray Painted Shades

Unfortunately, many of us learned to weld a can of spray paint under the watchful eye of someone who believed that the only right way to spray paint is to work right up close, covering the surface with a thick, even coat. Many professional artists work quite the opposite, holding the spray can several feet back and trying for an uneven misting of color instead. Their technique is simple to master and yields stunning results.

For the star shade, mist an ivory or white shade with a base color. Allow the base coat to dry. Cut out a dozen star shapes from heavy paper and tape them around the shade from their back sides. Mist the shade again with quick spurts of a darker color spray paint. Remove the stencils and allow the paint to dry. Add crescent moons and stars with a fine-tipped brush and gold paint, then embellish with the trim of your choice. (The antique black buttons used here were dabbed with hot glue over their sewing holes and then pressed in place.)

For the penny shade, coat a purchased shade with a solid tone of gold spray paint. After the paint has dried, add a mist coat of black spray paint from several feet away, turning as you spray to create an antiqued look. Add coins or any other trim with glue. (Note: Metal trims, such as coins, should be attached with an epoxy adhesive, not hot glue.)

For the cloud shade, cut out several cloud shapes from sturdy paper. Tape the shapes from their back sides to a purchased white fabric shade, then apply the blue color with light mists of spray paint. (Note: For a fuzzier edge to the cloud shapes, use larger balls of tape so that the stencil does not sit flush against the shade.) After the paint dries, hot-glue a gold lame sun and some bead trim (the trim on this shade was cut apart from a Christmas tree garland) around the top and bottom edges. See pages 108 and 113 for cloud and star motifs.

DESIGN: JONATHAN P. STUCKY

PAINTED SHADES

People who love to paint can't help but visualize lamp shades as prepared canvases. To create shades like the ones shown left, prepare the surface of a paper or fabric shade with enough coats of quick-drying spray primer to form an opaque surface. (The brush strokes will show through if you apply it with a brush.) After the primer dries, lightly transfer the design you plan to paint to the surface.

For these shades, the artist worked with oil paints because they allow for thinner washes and the drying times are much slower, providing more time for blending. The leaf shade shown right reveals a much thicker application of oil paints, which creates interesting lighting effects when the interior bulb is lit and enhances the painterly style of the work. For the two shades shown far left, acrylic paints were used.

DESIGN: LEE ANDRE, LEFT
DESIGN: MARION PECK, INSET

PLEATED CHIFFON SHADE

Simple pleats and gathers create an elegant, finished look to scallop-edged shades. To make the shade, line a shade frame or start with an existing shade. Measure the distance around the frame (the circumference) and the height. Cut out a rectangle of chiffon that is three times the circumference and 3" taller than the height.

Sew a narrow rolled hem along one short edge of the chiffon. Mark the center top and center bottom points in one panel with a washable fabric pen. Place the rolled edge at the marks with the fabric's right side facing out. Pleat or gather the chiffon by hand, filling the remaining half of the scallop's valley with as much fullness as desired. Pin in place.

Mark the center top and bottom points of the remaining panels. Smooth the bottom edge of the fabric over the form to the next valley, pinning to retain tension, then smooth the top edge of the fabric to the next mark and pin. Continue working from one center mark to the next until you reach the starting point. Trim off any excess fabric and roll-hem the raw edge. Pin in place, then slip stitch.

DESIGN: LEAH NALL

WORLD SHADE

Antique globes provide just the right shape and patterns for an interesting lamp shade. To make the shade, carefully cut a cardboard or laminated paper globe in half with a mat knife. Cut a length of 3/4" plastic tubing (available in a hardware store) to fit around the bare edge of the globe. Carefully cut a lengthwise opening in the tubing with the mat knife. (The tubing has a natural curve to it and following it as you cut will help it fit around the globe much better.) Spray paint the tubing in a complementary color. After the paint dries, spread the tubing open and fold it around the globe.

Use wire cutters to cut out a star shape with a hole in the center from a sheet of house flashing. Press decorative grooves into the flashing with a large nail if desired, then finish with a coat of spray paint. Work a hole into the top center of the globe with the pointed end of a screw. Position the star under the finial and assemble.

Wall sconces can be made from quartered globes with the same techniques. See page 107 for star pattern.

DESIGN: MARY JANE MILLER

GOLDEN THREAD SHADE

Transform sewing room scraps into a memorable shade in an afternoon. Begin by spray painting a narrow border around the top and bottom edges in gold paint. Do not try to make the border too precise — it should reflect the spontaneity of the threads. Allow the spray paint to dry completely.

Add small pieces of gold foil around the shade. Coat the shade with a thin layer of brush-on acrylic medium (gloss or matte), then press short strands of metallic thread in place. After the first layer of acrylic dries, finish with a second layer.

DESIGN: SANDY WEBSTER

PUFF PAINTED SHADE

Puff paints have been enchanting designers since their appearance on the craft market, and people are still coming up with new ways to use them. To make this shade, first decide whether you want to create a random or a repeating pattern. If you plan to make a repeating pattern, trace the surface area of the shade onto a piece of tissue paper. Divide the tissue paper into quadrants (or any other spacing unit) and plan your design to prevent awkward spacing. Apply the puff paints with an even hand. See page 107 for pattern.

DESIGN: KIM TIBBALS

COPPER MESH SHADE

Copper and other fine metal meshes can be used like fabrics to create beautiful shades with fascinating lighting effects. The metal meshes (similar to hardware cloth and screening but with a much finer weave) are used industrially for fine filter work, so you may need to seek out mail order companies to find a source.

To make the beaded shade, tape a piece of newspaper to fit the dimensions of your shade or lighting hardware. (For this shade, the designer made a pattern in the shape of a snug-fitting cone. He then added 3" to the bottom dimension to create a well-proportioned flare.) Untape the pattern and add $^1/_4$" to the top, bottom, and both sides. Make cutting marks for the strips in even intervals around the bottom and up about half of the shade's height. Cut out the pattern from the mesh.

Gently roll a hem down around the top edge, then finger press the side edges flat. Attach a length of fine-gauge copper wire to the top lip and weave it back and forth between the two sides, threading several transparent beads onto the wire with each crossover. Accordion-pleat the bottom strips and roll up a hem.

DESIGN: JONATHAN P. STUCKY

BATTENBERG LACE SHADES

Battenberg lace and crisp linen combine to create crisp, light lamp shades. To make the shade shown right, spray paint a six-paneled frame in white. Trace one panel section onto paper to create a pattern. Cut out three panels of fabric and finish their raw edges with a zigzag stitch. Cut out three panels of lace from the pattern, adding an extra inch to the bottom edge. Depending on the width of your panels, you may need to piece the lace sections. (A 10" shade will require approximately $1/4$ yard of linen and 3 yards of lace, washed and pressed.)

Pin the top edges of the fabric in alternating panels to the top edge of the frame. Position the lace in the remaining panels, allowing the extra inch to hang off the bottom edge. Secure the lace to the linen with fabric glue. Trim away any excess lace. Glue a lace border around the top and bottom edges, then glue the top linen edges to the frame.

To make the shade shown left, spray paint a six-paneled 6 - 7" high frame in white. Wash and press a purchased 14 x 20" Battenberg lace placemat. Measure and cut $8^{1}/2$" in from both outer edges of the long side, leaving a 3" center strip. Fold and cut the 3" strip in half to form two 3 x 7" pieces. Zigzag the raw edges of the two large pieces, then zigzag their corner edges, tapering at the top.

Trim away any excess fabric from the back side. Gather one long edge of each piece and pin them to the top of the frame, adjusting the threads to fit. Reinforce with fabric glue as needed.

DESIGN: JOYCE CUSICK

Refinished Glass Shades

Ordinary glass shades make a great surface to embellish with any number of creative techniques. If your shade has decorative sections or ribs, try to incorporate them into your design.

To make the mosaic shade, thoroughly wash and dry a glass shade. Mold strips of brown or gray polymer clay into sections on the shade, then oven bake on top of the shade as directed by the manufacturer. Allow the shade to completely cool.

Spread a thick layer of clear silicone glue over one section with a plastic knife. Press small pieces of colored glass or pebbles into the glue. Allow to set, then move on to the next section.

To make the striped shade, press a piece of paper between the raised ribs on a glass shade and mark the imprint lines. Cut out strips of metallic-finished tissue paper (brass and copper were used here) in the pattern shape.

Brush or sponge on a thin coat of matte finish decoupage medium to the back of the tissue paper and quickly press in place, gently smoothing out all wrinkles. After the tissue paper has completely dried, spray the entire shade with a coat of matte finish sealer. Finish by gluing a narrow trim onto the edges.

DESIGN: FRED GAYLOR

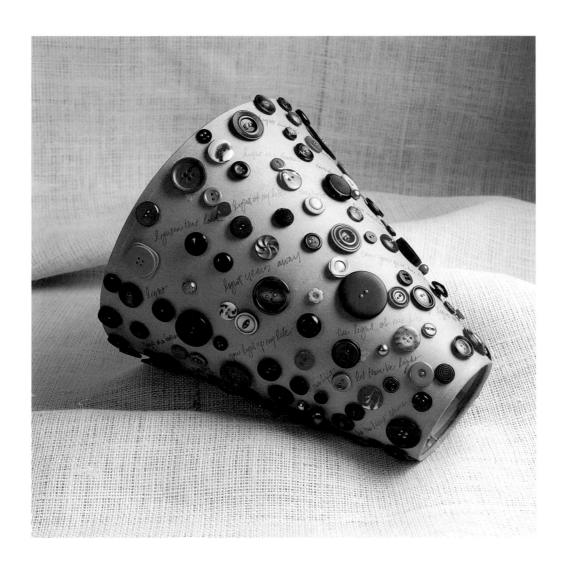

TRINKET SHADE

Inexpensive shades made from brown kraft paper can be found at larger home improvement stores, and make the perfect background for attaching small trinkets and collectibles. To make this shade, hot-glue an assortment of buttons, bottle caps, and anything else that appeals to you to the shade. (Note: If you don't want to risk damaging your items with glue, you can stitch them to the shade with a sharp-tipped tapestry needle.)

DESIGN: MARY McCLAREN

MICA SCONCE

This clever sconce was created from a simple hexagonal box and a mica woodstove window (available at hardware stores).

To make the sconce, cover the inside of an interesting cardboard box and deep-fitting lid with gold leaf. Cut an opening for the mica window with a craft knife. Cut an opening for the socket at the bottom and punch small venting holes near the top. Insert the socket. Glue a picture hanger on the center back of the box. Cut the mica a little larger than the window opening and attach it to the inside of the box lid with hot glue. Position the lid so that there is at least $^1/_2$" of clearance between the bulb and the mica window, then glue the lid in place.

DESIGN: PAT SCHEIBLE

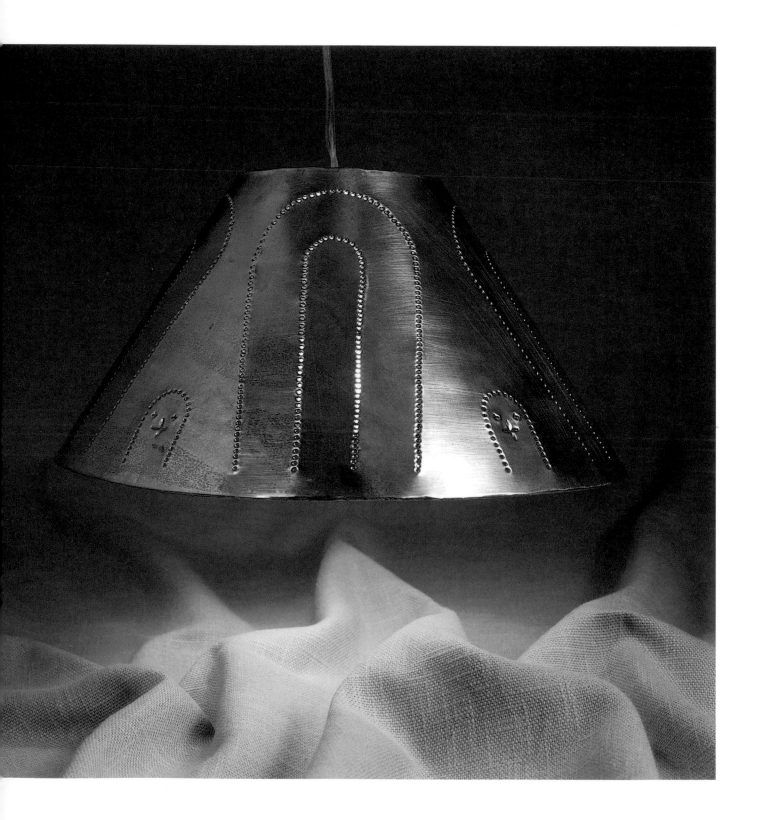

TIN SHADES

Tin makes a versatile material for a variety of lamp shades. It can be shaped, punched, and painted, just to name a few of the possibilities. To begin, make cone patterns from newsprint and tape them together until you're happy with a specific size and shape. Untape the cone, trace its shape onto a sheet of metal flashing, and cut it out with metal snips.

Transfer a pattern with sewing chalk onto the right side of the metal. Search around for objects to punch with. Nails create dots, while screwdriver tips will give you a line. Place your nail (or other punching object) on top of the pattern and hit it firmly with a hammer. Continue in this fashion until you've completed your design. To add color, spray the metal with a coat of primer, then spray paint. Glue a top fitter

ring inside the top of the cone or make short snips in the metal around the top in $1/4$" intervals and fold the metal's edge around the ring.

For the shades shown here, a morse code pattern, constellations, and a geometric pattern were punched into the tin. See page 107 for the geometric punching pattern.

DESIGN: BOBBY HANSSON, ABOVE
DESIGN: MARY JANE MILLER, OPPOSITE PAGE

88

REJUVENATED ANTIQUE LAMP

Damaged glass panels have sent many an antique lamp to the flea market. The panels are easy to replace; just be sure to choose colors and patterns in keeping with the shade's time period and style.

To begin the shade, carefully remove any re-maining glass panels. Spray the frame with a red oxide primer, then with the color of your choice. Trace each panel section to make a newspaper pattern, then cut out the panels from a sheet of framing plastic and from a decorative paper. Choose an inset shape and cut out a cardboard pattern. Trace the pattern onto each of the paper panels, then cut out the shape with a craft knife.

Brush a light layer of craft glue over the plastic panels and smooth the paper in place. Cut out the pattern shape from a con-trasting decorative paper and press the paper cutouts in place. Allow the glue to completely dry, then replace the panels.

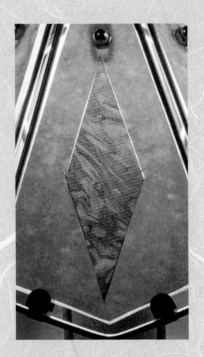

DESIGN: FRED GAYLOR

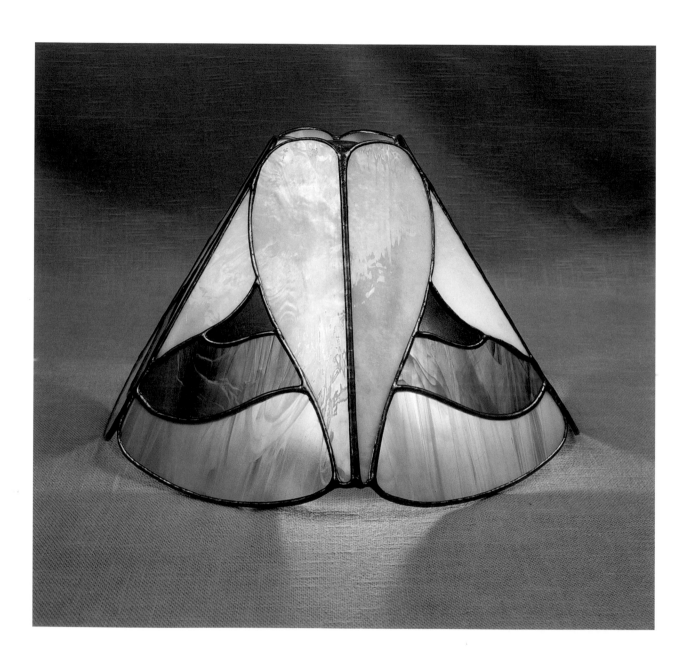

STAINED GLASS SHADES

Stained glass lighting has been enchanting the world for centuries, and the creative possibilities are virtually endless. If you're familiar with the basics of stained glass making, these shades should be fairly easy to assemble.

To make the truncated tetrahedron hanging lamp, begin by choosing a feature glass for panel A, a complementary glass for panels B and C, and a darker, accent glass for panel D. Cut and grind all panels. (See page 111 for panel patterns; enlarge as desired.) Copper foil and solder the three A-B-C panels at their front, back, top, and bottom edges. Foil and edge solder the D panels.

Tack three A-B-C panels together. Add a three-legged spider piece at the top of the B-C panels where they join. Solder the inside, then the outside of the remaining seams. Apply a copper patina and clean, then mount the electrical hardware and chain.

To make the leaf and blossom table-lamp shade, cut and grind glass pieces to fit the pattern. (See page 110.) Copper foil and solder the three right-hand and three left-hand panels at their front, back, top, and bottom edges. Tack and solder these six panels together. Solder a spider piece inside the top of the lamp at the inside and then the outside seams. Apply a copper patina and clean.

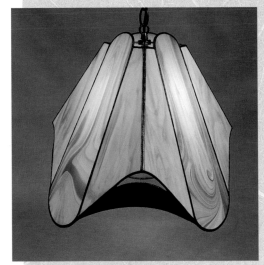

DESIGN: GENE MESSICK

GOURD LIGHTING

Gourds have been used as decorative, functional vessels for thousands of years. The surface of a dried gourd is very similar to wood, and can be painted, carved, burned, sculpted, and finished in any number of ways. Search for dried gourds at farmers' markets and roadside stands.

To make a gourd shade, begin by gently cleaning the outer layer of a dried gourd with sandpaper or a stainless steel pot scrubber. Gourds with stubborn dirt or mold may need to be held under warm water for several minutes before cleaning. Next, insert a kitchen knife through the gourd, then finish cutting with a keyhole saw or a craft knife. Some gourds will cut quite easily, while others will test your resolve.

If you plan to make a sconce, cut the gourd from the top stem down the side to the bottom. For a traditional shade, cut the gourd around its center, then cut out an opening for the hardware at the center top. For a candle cover or a combined shade and base, cut an opening in the center bottom large enough for the hardware to fit through.

Use a grapefruit spoon to clean out the dried pulp from inside the gourd. (Note: Some people are allergic to the pulp materials and should work outdoors and wear a breathing mask.) Purchase a fixture to fit inside your gourd and glue it in place with a multi-purpose glue.

Transfer your chosen motifs or patterns onto the gourd with carbon paper, chalk pens, or stencils. For dot patterns, make the holes with a drill, using an assortment of drill bits to create a variety of sizes. For cutout patterns, work slowly and carefully

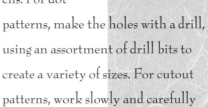

DESIGN: GINGER SUMMIT

with a craft knife, replacing the blades as they dull. Create painted designs with leather dyes, following the manufacturer's instructions. Gourds with unsightly blotches or holes can be repaired with plaster and then sprayed with several coats of texture paint. Other embellishment options include gold leafing and carving, to name just a few. Finish all gourds with a clear coat of varnish.

These night lights and strings of holiday lights illustrate some of the many lighting possibilities with gourds. To make night light, cut a small gourd sideways from its stem. Clean out the gourd and create the cutout designs. Add hints of color by painting the area around the cutouts from the inside of the gourd. Dye a simple plastic night light fixture to match the gourd with leather dye, then glue the gourd over the fixture.

For the holiday lights, carve out a small opening at the center bottom of a dozen or so gourds, then clean them out. Carve Christmas or Halloween cutout patterns in the gourds. Fit the bottom opening of each gourd over a bulb on a string of holiday lights and secure in place with poster adhesive. See pages 108 and 112 for patterns and motifs.

CROCHETED SHADE

There's more to crochet than baby blankets and afghans. The pattern on this shade is a free-form design, which can be intimidating to people who like rigid instructions. If you're unhappy with the way it's turning out, though, just unravel and start again.

To make the shade, closely wrap all frame edges of a multi-paneled frame with cream-colored yarn. The yarn will help hold your stitches in place as you work around the frame. Work the shade in single crochet stitches with a few slip stitches. Attach the yarn to the bottom edge of a panel. Single crochet across the panel, pulling up with the hook as you work, making two or three single stitches per inch. *Sl st to the other strut of the panel and turn. SC back to the other side, keeping tension on the hook so the new stitches will pull up on the previous row and all the stitches will be tight in the frame.

Vary the height of the rows by placing the sl st close to the last sl st or up to ³⁄₄" up the frame from the last sl st. Repeat from * three more times. Sl st to the frame, make two or three sl st down to the bottom right corner of the next panel and repeat the entire procedure. Keep going until you've crocheted in each panel. You can leave this yarn in place and sl st up to the next level when you're ready or tie it off. The sl sts will build up on the struts between the panels, and that's all right.

Attach a rainbow colored-yarn and work as you did for the cream-colored yarn. This time, turn the frame back and forth in the middle of some rows, so that the stitches build up at one side of the frame. For this shade, the frame was turned every time the yarn changed color. When enough rows are in one section (based on your intuition), work on the next panel. Follow your whims, keeping the stitches fairly tight on the frame. Continue in this fashion around the frame.

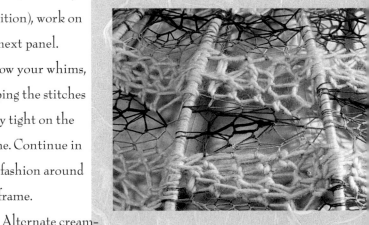

Alternate cream-colored sections with rainbow sections, decreasing the number of rows as the panels narrow. On the last round, when you've very close to the top of the frame, place some sts in the previous row, and some around the top of the frame. End off and turn in the ends.

Sew a lining to the top and bottom of the frame, tacking the lining as well as you can to each section about one-third up from the bottom. If you can, tack again one-fourth of the way down from the top. Finish by gluing a fringe trim around the bottom.

DESIGN: SUZANN THOMPSON

GOOSE EGG SHADE

A large goose egg creates a naturally glowing shade, while the twig cluster (purchased in a craft store) serves as a base and hides the wiring. To make the egg shade, carefully form ³/₈" holes in the top and bottom of the egg. (Note: If you don't have the patience to form little holes in delicate eggs, consider using a ceramic egg instead, many of which come with predrilled holes.) Gently work the last bulb on a string of small Christmas tree lights into the bottom hole and secure the light in place with small pieces of poster adhesive. Place the bulb in the center of the twigs and work the light cord discreetly out the back of the twig base.

DESIGN: PAT SCHEIBLE

IRIDESCENT SHADES

If you've always been attracted to colorful iridescent bows and tinsels, then you will love the way interior and exterior light affects this shade. To make the shade, loosely wrap a sheet of iridescent plastic film around a frame with interesting curves. Tentatively secure the top peaks with rubber bands.

Take the shade to a professional framer and ask her to apply heat to the film with the machine she uses to do shrink wrapping. Add a large drop of hot glue to the top of each peak, pulling to a peak, to form faux finials. Spray the inside of the shade with a flame retardant and choose a very low wattage bulb.

DESIGN: PAT SCHEIBLE

CUSTOM KNIT SHADE

Light shows off knitted lace motifs beautifully, giving the lace pattern the illusion of greater depth. In this shade, the lace holes let the most light through, while the popcorn stitches block the light almost completely. Even the areas of stockinette and reverse stockinette change the character of the light that comes through.

To make the shade, first make a swatch on 27" size 4 circular needles. Cast on 43 stitches (a multiple of 10 stitches plus 3) with bedspread cotton held double. Knit rows 1 - 20 two or three times, repeating between *s as necessary. Measure across two motifs in the middle of the swatch for approximate gauge.

Measure the width of one panel of a six-sided shade frame. Assuming that your knitted lace repeat is between 1³/₄" and 2¹/₄" wide, determine how many repeats will fit across the panel, then divide the panel width by the number of repeats you thick will fit across. This will give you the width your repeats should be. (For example, if your panel is 8"

across, about four repeats would fit across. Eight inches divided by four repeats is 2" per repeat. So when you knit your gauge swatch, aim for about 2" per repeat. If you can't achieve exactly 2" per repeat, go for a narrower gauge (less than 2" per repeat) because your knitting will stretch.)

To determine the number of stitches to cast on, multiply 6 (number of panels) by the num-

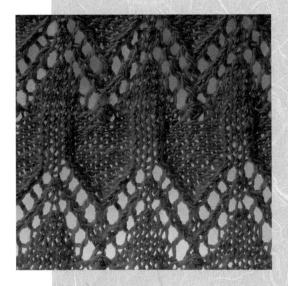

ber of repeats per panel by 10 stitches per repeat. In the example above, you would multiply 6 by 4 x 10 to equal 240 stitches to cast on.

Using bedspread cotton held double, cast on to circular needles. Joining to make a circle, making sure the stitches are not twisted. (Note: Your shade will have two or three struts holding the cen-

DESIGN: SUZANN THOMPSON

ter section to the frame. These instructions are written so that your knitted hem will flow over the struts. If desired, you can divide your cast on, knit separate sections back and forth so the hem splits around the struts, then join your knitting into a circular piece on the last row before the pattern starts.)

To make the top hem, knit 3 rounds and purl 1 round. Begin knitting the pattern stitch, repeating the 20 pattern rounds until the piece is long enough to fit the height of the shade without too much stretching or bunching. Purl 1 round and knit 3 rounds for the bottom hem. Bind off an darn in ends.

Line the shade frame. Pull the knitted cover over the lined frame so that the struts between the panels line up with K3 sections of the pattern. Pin the hem around the top and bottom of the frame so the purl row is at the edge of the frame. Sew down the hem.

PATTERN STITCH FOR SWATCH:

Rows 1, 3, and 5 (right side): k 3, * p 7, k 3 *.

Rows 2, 4, and 6: p 3, * k 7, p 3 *.

Row 7: k 2, * yo, ssk, p 5, k2tog, yo, k 1 *, end k 1.

Row 8: p 4, * k 5, p 5, *, ending last repeat p 4.

Row 9: k 3, * yo, ssk, p 3, k2tog, yo, k 3 *.

Row 10: p 5, * k 3, p 7 *, ending last repeat p 5.

Row 11: k 2, * (yo, ssk) twice, p 1, (k2tog, yo) twice, k 1 *, end k 1.

Row 12: p 6, * k 1, p 9 *, ending last repeat p 6.

Row 13: k 3, * yo ssk, yo, sl1-k2tog-psso, yo, k2tog, yo, k 3 *.

Rows 14, 16, and 18: purl all sts.

Row 15: k 4, * yo, ssk, k 1, k2tog, yo, k 5 *, ending last repeat k 4.

Row 17: k 5, * yo, sl1-k2tog-psso, yo, k 7 *, ending last repeat k 5.

Row 19: k 3, * p 3, (k 1, p 1, k 1, p 1, k 1) in next st, then pass the 2nd, 3rd, 4th, and 5th sts on right-hand needle separately over the last st made; p 3, k 3 *.

Row 20: p 3, * k 7, p 3 *.

PATTERN STITCH FOR LAMPSHADE COVER:

Rounds 1 through 6: k 2, * p 7, k 3 *, p 7, k 1.

Round 7: * k 1, yo, ssk, p 5, k2tog, yo *.

Round 8: k 3, * p 5, k 5, *, p 5, k 2.

Round 9: * k 2, yo, ssk, p 3, k2tog, yo, k 1 *.

Round 10: k 4, * p 3, k 7 *, p 3, k 3.

Round 11: * k 1, (yo, ssk) twice, p 1, (k2tog, yo) twice *.

Round 12: k 5, * p 1, k 9 *, p 1, k 4.

Round 13: * k 2, yo, ssk, yo, sl1-k2tog-psso, yo, k2tog, yo, k 1 *.

Rounds 14, 16, and 18: knit all sts.

Round 15: * k 3, yo, ssk, k 1, k2tog, yo, k 2 *.

Round 17: * k 4, yo, sl1-k2tog-psso, yo, k 3 *.

Round 19: k 2, * p 3, (k 1, p 1, k 1, p 1, k 1) in next st, then pass the 2nd, 3rd, 4th, and 5th sts on right-hand needle separately over the last st made (this makes a popcorn); p 3, k 3 *, p 3, make a popcorn, p 3, k 1.

Round 20: k 2, * p 7, k 3 *, p 7, k 1.

Repeat rounds 1–20 for pattern.

Fun-Fur Shade

An assortment of animal knicknacks inspired this shade for a child's room. To make the shade, make a paper pattern for each section of a multipaneled shade frame. Add a ¼" seam allowance to all sides and cut out the pattern in faux fur. Clip ¼" off each corner. Pin the sections together with right sides facing and stitch the side seams.

Turn right side out and whipstitch the upper edge to the frame. Repeat with the bottom edge, stretching the fabric taut as you work. Stretch the fabric around a metal strut from the inside, encasing the strut in the stretched fabric. Pin securely, then stitch with a zipper foot or by hand with a running stitch and quilting thread. Repeat with the remaining side struts, then sew on beads and other trinkets.

DESIGN: JONATHAN P. STUCKY

SPONGED SHADE

A creative application of craft paint can transform inexpensive vinyl shades into custom creations in less than an hour. To make this shade, squirt three colors of puff paint onto a piece of cardboard and dilute them a little with water. (The designer for this used bronze, gold, and turquoise to create an oxidized effect.) Scrunch a small sea sponge in your hand to shape it into a circle. Dip the sponge into the paint. Vary the colors you choose, sometimes using a single color, sometimes two, and sometimes dipping the sponge in all three colors. Twist the sponge in a circular motion as you apply it. When the paint dries, glue a length of woven black braid around the top and bottom edges, then glue a length of gold cording on top of the braiding.

DESIGN: KIM TIBBALS

SILK FOLIAGE SHADES

Here's a simple way to convert a garage sale find into a fun shade. Begin by removing the leaves from several stems of silk foliage. Attach the leaves to the shade with a cool-melt glue gun. For best results, start at the top of the shade, folding the top third of the leaves down inside the shade to form a finished top edge. Work your way down at an angle, overlapping as you go, allowing some of the lower leaves to dangle over the edge.

DESIGN: MARY JANE MILLER, RIGHT
DESIGN: FRED GAYFOR, LEFT

FUR SHADE

Here's a surprisingly simple way to recycle an antique fur coat. (Or search out a small piece of fun fur at a fabric store.) Start with a small old shade in a simple shape. Spray paint the inside of the shade gold or cover it with gold leaf. Wrap the collar portion around the shade, trim off any excess fur, and hot glue in place. Trim the edges with gold braid.

DESIGN: PAT SCHEIBLE

PATTERNS & MOTIFS

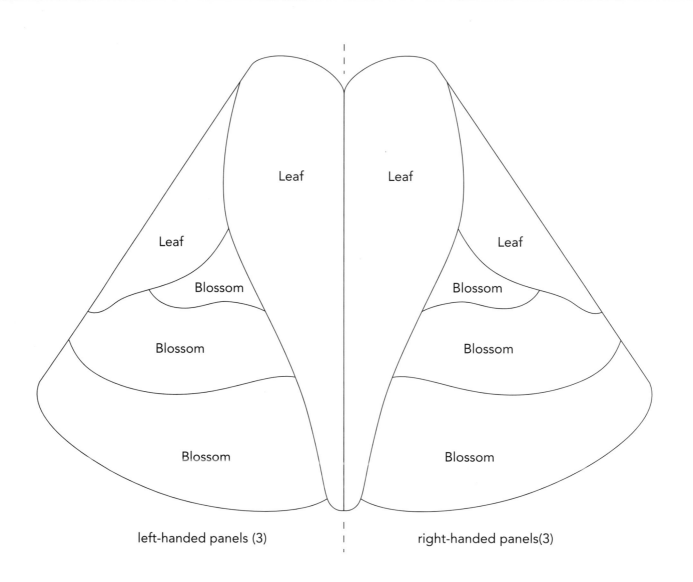

Leaf   Leaf

Leaf   Leaf

Blossom   Blossom

Blossom   Blossom

Blossom   Blossom

left-handed panels (3)   right-handed panels(3)

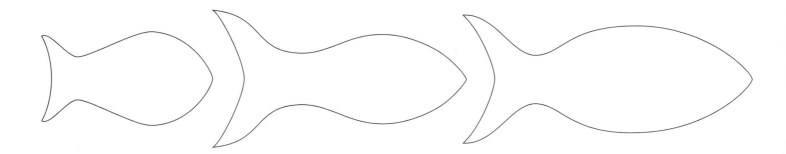

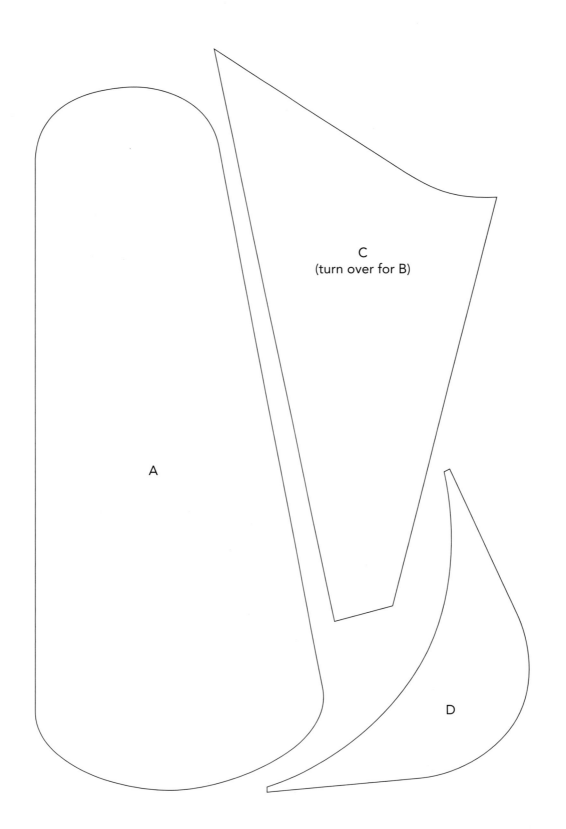

A

C
(turn over for B)

D

ANDREW OLSEN

PHOTO: LEE BRAUER

PHOTO: LEE BRAUER

"I graduated with a painting degree but couldn't find studio space, so I ended up working in a cabinet shop," says artist Andrew Olsen. "One day at work I stumbled across lighting when I held a piece of veneer up to the light." Andrew's pieces are constructed by a frame and panel technique, which allows the veneer to expand and contract without splitting.

"I've always had a thing for geometry, and my pieces are very mathematical. My earlier works were usually linear because that was the experience I had with wood, but curved lines really appeal to me and they've become easier to execute."

— *Andrew Olsen*
— Andrew Olsen

WILLIAM C. RICHARDS

"Art is more a verb than a noun," says lamp shade maker William Richards, who began his career as an artist in his father's shop building fantasy items such as a scuba tank made out of juice cans. "Art is a problem-solving process — it doesn't necessarily have to be a pretty picture to hang on a wall."

Will's formal training is in ceramics, and he works primarily with large ceramic wall plates and panel systems. "My shades began as opposition to the clean, symmetrical shades sold in stores. They are made with a composite, epoxy fabric that cures after it's been formed around an object, and the bases are pit fired stoneware." William searches out old boilers and other interesting items in the dump for mould mandrels.

"The assembly process is very quick and spontaneous. The shades create a very warm light, and I really enjoy how they can be arranged and hung together in so many different ways." Will does limited production work for interior designers and larger custom projects on occasion.

— *William C. Richards*
Clay Canvas Designs

CARTER CLOUGH

"My designs originate from my love of the American Arts and Crafts period," says artist Carter Clough. A strong desire to emulate nature in a functional, artistic medium emerged after many years as a photographer. "My commercial assignments required studying interiors and observing objects and their relationship to lighting and space." Curiosity led Carter to experiment, creating simple furniture pieces as exercise. Later, as he became more intrigued, he gave up photography. "My hobby became an obsession."

Today, Carter designs hand-built metal furniture and lighting with materials such as rawhide combined with steel and copper with rusted and faux finishes. Carter adds additional color by flame torching and with a variety of chemical and other finishes. Often described as Gothic or medieval, Carter's work involves minute detail work. Each Torchiere lamp, for example, requires drilling and threading 72 screws by hand. "Creating and completing an idea, and watching as the piece evolves is what my work is all about."

— *Carter Clough*
Carter Clough Furniture Design and Production

BILLY HALL

"In the beginning, I was so intrigued with how the light looked coming through wood shades that I didn't care what they looked like the rest of the time. After talking with lots of customers, though, I've come to realize that the daytime aspect to wood lamps is very important to people," says lamp shade maker Billy Hall. "The light that comes through the wood at night is a soft, deep light, while the light reflecting off the shade during the day is completely different."

Billy left a career in protein biochemistry after an extended vacation with a woodworker. "I was so intrigued with how much detail there is in wood. One night I was working in my studio and shaved off an end grain by mistake. I noticed that light was coming through the wood. It was totally unexpected — I had never associated translucency with wood." Billy spent six months trying to turn wood thin enough to make a lamp shade on a lathe, and another 18 months learning to stabilize the wood for heat. "I want my work to show people the history of a tree, every season and every storm in magnificent chemical detail."

— *Billy Hall*
Glowing Wood Sculptures

NORMAN BACON

PHOTO: PETER KRICKER

"Art for the home is a passion of mine," says ceramic artist Norman Bacon. "Lighting is special because of the ambiance that it can create. The light emanating from a ceramic shade highlights the subtleties of the surface while casting a warm copper glow into the surrounding space.

"I chose ceramics as my medium after discovering the joy and spontaneity of working with clay. When you are a ceramicist you can't help living in the moment. The elements are at your fingertips and the moment is magic." Raku, the technique Norman uses, originated in Japan in the late 1500s, and involves rapid firing and a well-controlled cooling. "For me, the Raku process is expressed most exquisitely in the split-second transformation of the materials after I've surrendered my control. When I crouch before the fire imagining the results, it feels as though something is about to be born, and then, in a moment, a wonderful work happens."

— *Norman Bacon*
— Norman Bacon Studio

OLIVIER ROLLIN

"In my designs, a lamp is not necessarily separated into a shade and a base. They are one, and together they work like a piece of sculpture," explains French multimedia artist Olivier Rollin.

"My formal education was in industrial design, which stresses the importance of designing everything in advance, down to the most minute details. My first clay lamps were executed that way, but I later preferred to be more spontaneous."

Olivier's paper shades are formed in layers over a mold with reinforcing reeds arranged between the layers for support. "There are all kinds of things happening with the paper itself, so it's a very spontaneous medium." The reeds extend out from the bottom of the shade and go into a weighted base. "I'm most interested in what the light will do for the layers of paper, and I've started working with transparent molds so I can better control the lighting effects during construction."

— *Olivier Rollin*
Olivier Rollin Designs

LISA GRAVES

"Copper is a good material to work with," says multimedia artist Lisa Graves. "It's soft and very malleable, which allows me to make shades primarily by hand." Originally a jewelry designer, Lisa veered off first into candlesticks and then into other types of lighting. "I try to make lamps and shades that are like jewels for the home, so I use a lot of glass and copper.

Lisa markets her work through wholesale gift and furniture shows, and really enjoys doing production work. "Even though I'm creating the same piece, the shades vary a lot from one another, and I really like the small imperfections that make them subtly different from each other."

— *Lisa Graves*
ASIL

PHOTO: DAN CLARK

GENE MESSICK

"Glass has always fascinated me," says stained and fused glass artist Gene Messick. "The transparency of color with light coming through it is so intriguing." Most of Gene's glass pieces combine his love of natural forms with a strong geometric component from his professional background as an industrial designer.

Many of Gene's favorite shades are made of fused glass, an ancient medium dating back nearly 4,000 years. "Fused glass is a fairly complex process, but it's very intriguing because it gets rid of the lead line and allows you to add color next to color without interruption. Fused glass offers all sorts of wonderful lighting applications."

— *Gene Messick*
Lightworks Studio

JUDY DYSTRA-BROWN
BOB BROWN

Granite river boulders, branches, rattan, bamboo, and handmade paper are the elements of Bob Brown and Judy Dykstra-Brown's light sculptures. "We strive for a fusion of nature and function with elegant, simple styling," says Judy. "Each piece is unique."

Hand carving tools, oil and water cooled diamond saws, grinders, and core drills are used to work the boulders. (The wiring passes through the wood and stone to keep it hidden in finished sculptures.) Bob and Judy make their shades by cooking and pounding mulberry bark to create pulp, which is then formed into paper on Japanese molds. Reeds and other natural materials are laminated between the layers, then sprayed with flame retardant and sealer, stretched, and attached to a superstructure.

— Judy Dystra-Brown
— Bob Brown

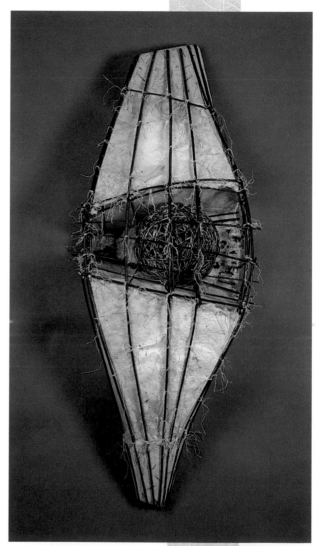

Sue Johnson

"For me, the trick is being able to balance the creative part of professional lamp shade design and production with the business part," says lighting artist Sue Johnson. Sue's shades are made from thin sheets of pressed mica, and she enjoys being part of a tradition that reportedly began in the late 1800s when light sources were powered by both gas and electricity and shades needed to be adaptable to both.

"I love working with mica. If it doesn't sustain some horrendous catastrophe, it's very durable, and even very old shades can be repaired. It makes you feel good to be able to

make something that may last hundreds of years." Sue learned the basics of shademaking from a professional, but she fine-tuned her skills working alone. "To become a quality lamp shade maker, you just have to be willing to sit down and play with the materials until you figure it out."

— *Sue Johnson*
Sue Johnson: Custom Lamps and Shades

— *William Morris (bases)*

BEN GOLDSTONE
ADAM POLLOCK

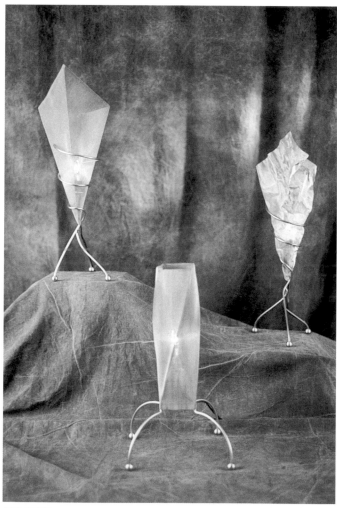

"Metal meshes are a really great material to work with," explains lighting artist Ben Goldstone. "The meshes are incredibly flexible — you can do just about anything with them. Some of the finer meshes are almost like silk." Ben began working with metal meshes while doing design work for the theater. "The light they give off has a very warm, romantic quality to it."

Ben and his partner, Adam Pollock, started their business five years ago in a garage, and their shades are sold through the wholesale market and are commissioned by architects and designers. "The shapes in our shades evolve pretty organically. Remarkably, many of the origami techniques I learned in Japan can be transferred to the meshes."

— *Ben Goldstone*
— *Adam Pollock*
Fire-Farm

ERIK VAN LENNEP

"I started making lamps ten years ago when I went shopping for new house lamps. I was appalled at the prices and insulted at the quality," says environmental artist Erik van Lennep. Many of Erik's lamp shades are created by layering leaves, dried flowers, grasses, pieces of hornets' nest, and architectural trace paper bonded with an acrylic polymer.

"The finished shades have a translucent quality to them. When the light bulb is off, there's only a hint of what's in there. When the light bulb is on, the light tends to be evenly diffused because of the optical quality of the materials. The yellow trace paper creates a very warm illumination, almost like a candle flame." Erik's shades are often nested or woven into a framework of branches and twigs. The shade shown here crowns a five foot paperbirch sapling, cut just days ahead of the power company's clippers. "I like to use the outdoors as my art-supply store. In that way, my pieces have a strong resonance with the character of my environment."

— *Erik van Lennep*
Native New England Design

PHOTO: GREG HUBBARD

LAURA GOLDBERG

"For this shade, I started working on the flat panels first, adding beads to a metal frame one at a time in the peyote stitch," explains bead artist Laura Goldberg. "The finished panels looked very stiff, though, so I added the beaded 'ruffles' to create more of a fabric illusion." Laura admits to being obsessed with beading. "There's so much tactile pleasure in beading, and the colors are so wonderful. It's just a really pleasing medium to work in."

A low wattage bulb displays the shade to its best advantage. "With the bulb off, you notice the different shapes and forms of the designs in the panels. Some of the beads are lined with color while others are translucent, and with the bulb on, you see a wonderful array of color and light.

— *Laura Goldberg*
Laura Goldberg Designs

PHOTO: ED ERNST

CYNTHIA WYNN

PHOTO: EVAN BRACKEN

"This lamp just seemed to come together one day when I was stacking some industrial scrap metals in my shop," says lamp and furniture fabricator Cynthia Wynn. "The grid patterns throw very intriguing and intense shadows. Initially, though, the lamp looked like a scrap metal Tiffany, and it really needed something else. Then a friend, Xanath Espina, showed me the glass beads she'd been making.

"There's such variety in Xanath's beads, and you can just look at them and see that she's having fun. Wiring the beads to the lampshade seemed like an obvious choice. We started with about a hundred beads, which we thought would be more than enough, but it actually took more than 300."

— *Cynthia Wynn (lamp)*
6 Riverside Studios
— *Xanath Espina (glass beads)*